The Watson Drawing Book

THE WATSON DRAWING BOOK

By Ernest W. Watson and Aldren A. Watson

BELL PUBLISHING COMPANY, INC.   NEW YORK

*This edition published by Bell Publishing Company, Inc.,
a division of Crown Publishers, Inc., by arrangement
with Reinhold Publishing Corporation*

C D E F G H

PRINTED IN THE UNITED STATES OF AMERICA
Library of Congress Catalog Card Number 62-19491

The AUTHORS *affectionately dedicate this book to* Nancy Dingman Watson

CONTENTS

Preface

THE PURPOSE

This book has been created for many people of all ages who, possessed by the urge for personal expression in the arts, may welcome a mentor to help them discover the pleasantest and most practical means of satisfying their creative hungers. It has been written not only for students seriously eager to learn to draw. It is addressed also to those who seek merely the ability to say something pictorially, to acquire another language. This may sound paradoxical but there are important differences in these objectives. The serious student may well be seeking professional competence, whether or not he hopes to earn his livelihood with pencil or brush. The others may be thinking of drawing as an adjunct to the written and spoken word, satisfied to be amateurs, albeit with a noticeable accent, and encouraged in the knowledge that a degree of awkwardness in pronunciation and syntax is not without charm.

The readers in this latter category are in good company. There are thousands who draw as a pastime. In the letters of many famous and not-so-famous persons we often find marginal sketches that enliven the pages and give point to the written message. Innumerable amateurs carry sketchbooks in their pockets when they set out upon a journey. Anyone can learn to draw well enough to serve such purposes; actually it is easy until one becomes tempted to dig deep into the profundities of art expression. Then the search for artistic verities can well lead one into the kind of dedication seen in the words of Hokusai, the Japanese master, who exclaimed, as he was dying at the age of 90, "If heaven would grant me ten more years or even five, I might still become a great artist."

The authors—assuming their readers to be somewhat less consecrated—have tried to guide the novice along the smoothest paths, while providing stairways for the more professionally-minded travelers to climb. The path is easier for today's beginner; he can set out with greater confidence than his predecessor of a generation ago. He has seen enough of contemporary art to understand that the desire for expression takes precedence over the demand for factual accuracy. Indeed he will find little concern with the latter in modern art. How many times has the gallery visitor said to a companion, "My eight-year-old could do as well as that," and in many instances he is right. The fact is that the essential characteristics of a subject can better be expressed by sketchy action than by meticulous delineation. A characteristic pose of the body, tilt of the head, or gesture of an arm without obvious reference to anatomical structure can often portray reality better than a more conscious awareness of the body's mechanical articulation. Of course it would be a mistake to imply that ignorance of anatomy and detail is a virtue, but a point we are making is that the relative beginner need not wait for hard earned proficiency before expecting to make very satisfying sketches. It is the natural tendency to be concerned with *details* that we are discouraging; that is why this admonition is being repeated throughout the text.

Before undertaking any journey, travelers want to know something of both the delights and hardships likely to be encountered along the way. Each route presents its own problems as well as its particular pleasures; not everyone will find the same itinerary congenial to his inclination or to his capabilities. This he well knows, so he consults maps and guidebooks. The present volume is offered as a guidebook for the artist in quest of pleasure in the graphic arts. It attempts to survey the territory and it instructs the wayfarer in the preparation for his adventures.

Although the term "graphic" in the dictionary is practically synonymous with "pictorial," in the art profession it refers specifically to the drawing arts and is not applied to the art of painting. Since drawing is the basis of all the graphic arts, the authors call this a drawing book. Drawing is implicitly an essential aspect of painting but the art of painting is a world of its own and it has a logical separation from the areas of representation with which we are now concerned. This is not to say that the painter is immune to the kind of instruction here offered; except for the technical methods which the reader will find here, the instruction in this book is like-wise useful to painting students. But of course it stops short of color problems, painting techniques, and the esthetic profundities related to the painting arts.

It is not expected that any reader will want to become involved in all the drawing techniques demonstrated on these pages; each person will instinctively be attracted to one, or to some. Our purpose is to display them all in the showcase, as it were, to encourage each to make his choice, either by instinct or by experimentation. The technical specimens shown in the various mediums are only samples; it is impossible to treat each technique exhaustively in a single book. Nearly all of the techniques might well be and indeed are subjects of separate books, some of which the serious student will want to consult after he has discovered his own preferences.

One of the first things to understand is that every one of us is different; hence, there is no one *right way* to draw. If we consider art a language of expression, each person has something personal to say and each must express himself in an individual way. Actually, as psychologists point out, nothing looks the same to any two people. And certainly none of us feels exactly the same as anyone else about anything. That is one of the exciting facts about life and art.

Some people think and work best in line; others in mass. Some prefer the flexible charms of pencils, others are temperamentally disposed to the vigor and directness of ink, either with the brush or pen. The brush—in wash technique—has its special appeal to other dispositions; and felt brush, a relative newcomer in the drawing field, will most congenially respond to a different personality. So do not expect to be equally proficient in all drawing techniques.

As will be pointed out in a later chapter, fear is the first enemy to be overcome. You must remember that you are the only person to be pleased with what you do; and if you judge your success principally by the fun you get out of drawing you should get a kick out of your earliest attempts, long before you consider yourself "proficient." The very feel of the pencil, the pen, or the crayon as it makes its first strokes on a clean sheet of paper ought to be an esthetic pleasure. And so it is!

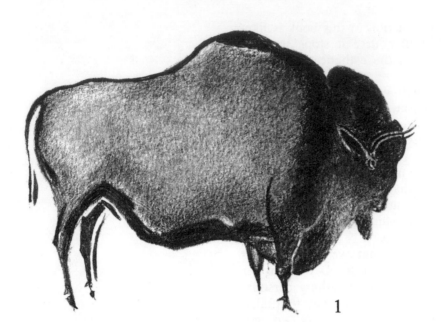

1

2

1 In the evolution of man, one of the earliest manifestations of his awakening intellect was the persistent urge to draw. In the caves of Europe are many drawings by paleolithic men, whose work displayed a surprising knowledge of anatomy and skill in esthetic representation. The painting of a bison on a cave wall in Spain is unusually realistic as well as expressive.

2 The Stag Hunt, a mural painting by a Stone Age artist, in the "Cueva de los Caballos" near Albocacer, Castellon, Spain.

3 Drawing by Noel Patrick Quinn, son of Noel Quinn, noted painter of the West Coast. The lad was 9 years old when this drawing was made.

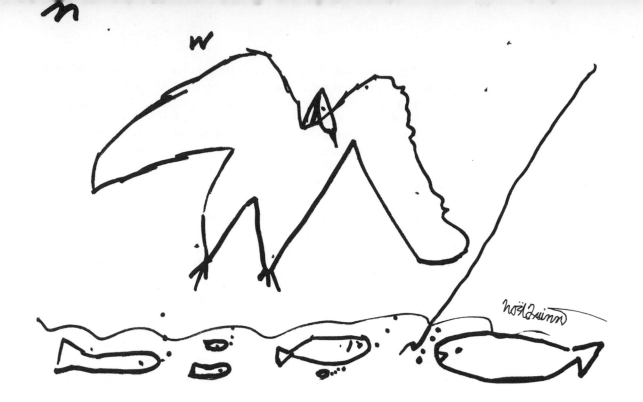

I *The Urge to Draw*

Almost everyone has, or has had, the urge to draw. Many adults have forgotten it, but drawing once came to them as naturally as eating. While some, to be sure, are more creative and articulate than others, every child draws. He keeps at it until with advancing years he becomes acquainted with the sophistication of professional drawing, grows self-conscious and discovers that he "can't draw." That is very sad! If someone had been around to disabuse him of that notion he might not have had to wait until becoming a grown man to realize how mistaken that idea was. Now, at an advanced age, whether twenty or sixty, the primitive urge often breaks out. He sees a lot of people now drawing and painting for no other objective than the fun of doing it; just as many are playing musical instruments with no thought of profit other than joy to their souls.

And what profit can be more satisfying than that? Today, more and more people are practicing some form of art for just that reason. They have nothing to sell; they have no customers to please other than themselves. However, they are not necessarily easy to please; as a matter of fact they can, in time, come to be pretty tough customers, increasingly demanding of their own creativeness and skills.

Drawing, as we have said, is an instinctive human expression. The impulse to draw is actually the first point of difference between the human child and animal young with which his unconscious development has grown apace. It is the first sign of creativity. Drawing of course is universally practiced by primitive people. With them it may not be an intentional art form, though often, perhaps inevita-

4

Action drawing from a Disney film.

bly, it becomes that. Those marvelous prehistoric pictures painted on the walls of caves were, we are told by students of anthropology, created to serve the most practical needs; pictures of the hunt, for example, being in effect either prayers for the hunter's success in the field, or the celebration of it. Also, then as now, picture images had their function in the practice of religion. In Egyptian art we can see how pictures were the origin of nonrepresentative symbols that eventually became the characters with which abstract thoughts could be expressed.

But the development of abstract symbols has not lessened the usefulness of pictures in the communication of ideas and the expression of those imponderables which are beyond the reach of speech and letters. Music, the dance, handicrafts—all art forms are in this category of communication through feeling and experience. Even bodily gestures are a form of drawing; they convey in motion an emphasis beyond the power of verbal expression. We all have imponderables to express in one or more of these arts; even in so simple an act as the drawing of a flower we release some part of our potential creativeness, which otherwise would remain imprisoned in our subsconscious. The person who has not experienced this kind of emotional release has no conception of the power there is in it for pleasantly transcending the day-by-day impact of mundane affairs. This is true no matter how amateurish the drawing may be. It is in the doing of it rather than in the result. From this point of view drawing is not necessarily an endowment of culture. That is proved by the uninstructed drawings of children. Even the crudest drawing, if it is done with feeling, becomes a significant contact with reality.

We have much to learn from children. They draw and paint without the fear that often grips the adult beginner, hesitant to put down his first stroke on paper. The expression "there is nothing to fear but fear itself" made memorable by a former president of the United States, applies to the early efforts of any student. When a layman is urged to "take up" picture-making in any form he may exclaim, "Why I can't even draw a straight line!" not realizing that drawing a straight line is seldom expected of him unless he is thinking of a very mechanical kind of delineation. The saying is merely a symptom of a general fear that he cannot draw anything at all. Thus the fear complex is the first stumbling block to be overcome. The conquering of that fear is the initial victory to be won. It can be achieved very quickly by the determination to spoil, intentionally, a great deal of paper. Start with the cheapest paper and the cheapest material. Just splash around with charcoal, ink, or crayon—any material at all. Don't even try to make a decent drawing, merely get acquainted with the feel of your medium and discover something of its nature. For example, with a stick of soft charcoal make rapid sketches of any object in the kitchen or a spray of flowers from the garden. Work on a large scale at first, using arm movement rather than finger movement. The results will be startling from the viewpoint of expression even though lacking accuracy

5

5   A brush and ink drawing by Kane Tanyu, famous Chinese artist who died in 1746.

6   Spontaneous brush and ink drawing by Ora Edwards, contemporary American, whose drawings of children are noteworthy.

7   Drawing by Laszlo Krauss, an orchestra conductor who calls drawing his "second love." This is a sketch of a musician in his orchestra.

7

6

8

Ballet Dancer Tying Her Shoe, by Edgar
Degas, French, 1834-1917.

9

Detail of an on-the-spot sketch by the late
Mahonri Young, a famous American sculptor, 1877-1957. Although he drew and sculp-
tured the human figure with great perception
and skill, in this sketch he merely recorded
a rapid note to be used later, perhaps in a
finished work.

10

in delineation of form. This is a "limbering-up" exercise that will give confidence and help to abolish timidity.

One cause of the beginner's timidity is the notion that without the ability to draw what he sees with precision and accuracy, his drawings have little value. A precise drawing can indeed be good; but precision, far from being an inevitable virtue, is often less inspired than an impulsive sketch that succeeds in endowing the subject with life. A fine example of this is the quill pen drawing of a lion by Eugène Delacroix (page 74), who could be very precise when he wished. Hendrik W. Van Loon, on the other hand, couldn't be precise. Although not a professional artist he could and did draw with both expression and information. He filled his books with sketches that give delightful graphic accompaniment to his written words even though they display lack of technical mastery. One might characterize his sketches as graphic gestures. (See his book *The Arts,* Simon & Schuster, 1937).

In a magazine article "Two Loves Have I" (*American Artist* magazine, January 1960) Laszlo Krauss tells what drawing does for him as an adjunct to his musical career. "As a musician and conductor I am a product of Europe. I never studied art in Europe. When I came to this country in 1947, one of my first jobs was with the Pops Concert Orchestra in Carnegie Hall. I could speak scarcely a word of English. In order to establish contact with my colleagues I started to make drawings of them. To their surprise and mine, all of the drawings were good likenesses if not masterpieces." These experiences led Mr. Krauss to such art study here as he finds time for. He draws when on tour—in concert halls, on stage, while traveling, and from hotel windows wherever he happens to be. Drawing has indeed enriched his life with another love.

Even such a master draftsman as the late Mahonri Young in his sketch "The Winner" [FIGURE 10], doubtless made on the spot in the moment of action, was content to express only the dramatic action without concern for anatomical accuracy. An accomplished artist can, even in rapid sketching, reveal his complete knowledge of the figure in action as in the same artist's ink sketch of the fighter standing over his fallen opponent [FIGURE 9].

Artists who make such casual sketches do not do so because of inability to draw with meticulous accuracy when that is desirable. The serious amateur will strive to develop his knowledge and his technical skill as rapidly as possible. The point we have been making is that one need not wait until his work begins to look professional before getting a lot of satisfaction out of it. Do not despise the first crude efforts. If the sketches look somewhat cockeyed so do many by the old masters, although their careless appearing drawings, we have to admit, give evidence of far greater knowledge and power of expression.

a.　　　　b.　　　　c.

11 The first two drawings, obviously the same pitcher, were traced from two different paintings by Eric Isenburger, contemporary painter; the third drawing (c) is a factual representation of his model. The fourth, (d) is reproduced from a detail in a figure composition by Andree Ruellan, a contemporary painter. Hers is an expressive rather than a factual drawing.

d.

Design enters into it; and that becomes a very subtle thing which we won't go into at this point, except to say that distortion such as we see in the drawings of the several pitchers [FIGURE 11] is often more interesting than perfect symmetry. In the meantime the beginner need not feel discouraged if his distortions are the result of incompetence rather than intention. It is better that his drawings often be expressive, though distorted, rather than painfully accurate and uninteresting. Nevertheless, all serious students should take some time for the discipline of facsimile reproduction. Every competent artist needs the kind of mastery earned by such discipline to enable him to draw with abandon. It might be a good idea, after drawing an object—the pitcher, for example—in a "reckless" manner, to draw it again as meticulously exact as possible.

Drawing may rightly be thought of as another "eye" because it enlarges the vision so enormously. When we draw an object we actually see much about it that would otherwise be unnoticed. Human vision is considerably more than a mechanical phenomenon. The brain is a more important part of it than the lens; the eye really sees only what we are curious enough to investigate. When we speak of the *trained eye*, we mean the trained brain. Everyone knows that two persons who observe the same scene or the same occurrence will bear witness to different aspects of it. Some will have noticed more than others. One artist we know can draw from memory, with astonishing completeness, the details of a room in which he had been for only a few brief moments. Under the same circumstances an untrained eye would have a very fuzzy picture of the

12 Jan Cornelius Sylvius, portrait sketch by Rembrandt, Dutch, 1606-1669. Although this drawing ignores detail, it satisfies because it is based on knowledge and is expressive. It demonstrates the power of dramatic action which emphasizes essentials. National Gallery of Art, Washington, D. C., Rosenwald Collection.

room. The difference is between *wanting* to see and *training* oneself to see.

We like what William Saroyan wrote along this line. "Is there such a thing as creative looking? I am convinced of it. What constitutes such looking? Clarity, intelligence, imagination, admiration and love. You make a point of looking at the object, you look steadily and clearly, you see the object, you see it again, you see it again, you notice the true nature of it in its entirety and in its parts, you relate its reality to all reality, to all time and space and action, you admire its survival, and you love its commonness and its individuality." Well this may seem a bit esoteric, at the least, poetical, but that's all right; there is a message here in the penetration of its thinking that is relevant even for the novice.

Now the beginner need not wait too long to get the feel and the function of his third eye, the eye of the brain; even in his first drawings he may begin to appreciate its reality. While drawing a knot in an old tree trunk, for example, he will discover something of nature's rhythm in the encircling bark. A stone on a rocky beach will give him delight as his pencil traces the sinuous flow of lines that reveal its long ago, fluid state. The artist enters into communion with nature, identifies with it as soon as he experiences the sensations of the searching eye. That is his business; it is what makes him an artist. Thus the world enlarges, revealing more and more of the wonderful delights that lie within reach, only awaiting the desire to accept them.

13   Nagasaki 14 o'clock 1945   Barse Miller

Pen sketch by Barse Miller.

14   Picasso? No, this is not a Picasso. It comes
from ancient Phrygia in what is now Turkey.
It is one of many drawings scratched on
walls of buildings 2700 years ago.

15

16

II *What is Good Drawing?*

We judge a drawing good or bad in the light of our prejudices, which are the result of education and artistic sensibility. However, there are drawings, made by savages or children, by the sophisticated or the naïve, by the trained and the untrained, which have a timeless and universal quality that transcends individual judgment. Everyone has his private definition of good drawing. But because that definition is influenced by personal variations of intellectual outlook, a multitude of concepts results. The common one is that a drawing need have only exact delineation, that is a faithful representation of something seen, or have so-called good craftsmanship.

A better concept, which encompasses a broader field of artistic appraisal, is one in which there is verisimilitude but with a quality of workmanship that we may call *spiritual* to express a certain refinement and sensitiveness in drawing technique.

Then there is the good drawing which has slighted resemblance in favor of a synthesis or simplification. And finally there is good drawing which has left exactness out, or abolished resemblance altogether, but which appears to have been accomplished with feeling and so fluently that it is calligraphic in character. In effect a drawing that has become an invention and seems to be intuitively, almost unconsciously, produced. Kandinsky presented a concept that may be better understood by those who have achieved a degree of esthetic sophistication, but it does have validity; and it is appropriate to mention it now when we are trying to express the artistic truth that

15 Brush drawing by Birger Lundquist, Swedish illustrator, 1910-1952.

16 Line drawing by John Flaxman, English sculptor, 1755-1826.

17

19

in all seriousness any way is the right way so long as it is inspired by the creative spirit. He said, "Good drawing is drawing that cannot be altered without destruction of its inner value irrespective of its correctness as anatomy, botany or any other science."

The several drawings of garden still life are used to illustrate entirely different attitudes an artist, or different artists, may have in sketching even the simplest objects. Figure 17 shows a wholly objective desire to state the facts of the subject as faithfully as possible. The artist drew the objects in correct perspective and simulated the light-and-shade and value subtleties with careful attention to detail. This may be called the academic approach.

In Figure 18 the same group has been drawn in quite a different spirit. Here the artist quite evidently was more interested in expression than in exactitude. We get a feeling of the artist's delight in broad effects of form and light, and of somewhat less regard for photographic accuracy. Perspective facts are not ignored, though somewhat slightingly observed, and the rendering is free and spirited. From the standpoint of expression, this is undoubtedly a better drawing.

The sketch of the flowerpot in Figure 19, made with a broad-nib pen, shows far less concern with reality. The object merely supplied the artist with an excuse for swinging that pen in a kind of emotional spree.

When we turn to Figure 20 we come to something quite different. We note an almost complete disdain of photographic reality in favor of invention. Perspective fact has been violated intentionally and factual form has been warped to suit the artist's sense of design.

18

20

Likewise, the light-and-shade aspects of the object have been "used" rather than copied. This approach is more accurately described as *designing* rather than sketching, because, instead of letting his pencil or pen dance over the object lightheartedly—one might almost say automatically—each line, tone and shape was "thought out." A good example of this kind of expression is seen in Figure 22, the still life by Juan Gris, French master of the early twentieth century. It represents a common attitude in modern art.

In John Marin's watercolor [FIGURE 23] there is a wholly spontaneous expression in which verisimilitude is repudiated in favor of design and uninhibited painting. Feininger's "City" [FIGURE 21] certainly is not the representation of a place; it is a symbol of the way the artist was affected by the angularity and confusion of a modern metropolis. Charles E. Luffman's Chinese-inspired, brush drawing [FIGURE 24] sings of the sinuous flow of lines in mountain and plain. We can aptly compare both drawings to poems. If we accept the analogy, and Archibald MacLeish's assertion that "a poem should not *mean,* but *be,"* we come rather close to the significance of drawings of this kind.

It is appropriate now to ask why *you* want to draw. You may not have stopped to analyze the *why;* you simply have the urge to do it. But it is worthwhile raising the question because recognition of just what it is that motivated that urge will direct the way you approach drawing and determine the nature of the result.

Is your impulse toward *expression* or factual *delineation?* The chances are, though not necessarily, it is the former. Likely enough your first living model will be that much-loved cat—or perhaps a

21

22

21 Woodcut by Lyonel Feininger, American, 1871-1936. National Gallery, Rosenwald Collection.

22 Fruit Dish and Bottle, by Juan Gris, Spanish, 1887-1927. Conté crayon, 18 x 12. Museum of Modern Art.

23 Stonington—from Green Head, Maine, by John Marin, American, 1870-1953. Watercolor, 17¼ x 20½. The Metropolitan Museum of Art, Alfred Stieglitz Collection 1949.

24 Brush drawing by Charles E. Luffman, contemporary American.

23

dog. It is natural that you should find pleasure in drawing him; and you doubtless have something in mind other than an encyclopedic illustration to identify the breed. More likely you will want to portray him in that engaging pose he takes when begging for a tidbit, or crouching for a spring upon a grasshopper. It is *expression* you want, not *definition*. This may seem too obvious a truth to state. Nevertheless, it is worthwhile to urge you to keep the objective continuously in mind in order to avoid the common error of meticulously focusing upon details, one at a time, then expecting that "the sum of the parts is equal to the whole." In drawing, this does not work! Begin with expression, seeing the whole in form, or in action if it is a live model. Rough out your subject quickly in mass or in line. What details are needed can be added after you have got the impression. The drawings of the cock by Evaline Ness [FIGURE 29] show how a fine professional artist puts the emphasis on expresssion.

What the late Maurice Sterne once said in this connection is worth quoting: "Drawing which suggests playing the piano by note is obviously all wrong. You must not draw what you *see* but what you *have* seen. One cannot make a decent drawing while the vision is divided in seeing different parts at different times. Only when the vision is so coordinated that every part is seen in its true relationship to the rest, has one the right to indulge in drawing."

The teaching methods of Hoyt L. Sherman at the Ohio State University are worth mentioning in connection with the approach to perceptive seeing. It is *drawing by seeing*. We can only refer here to one aspect of the method, the basic one really, which dramatically teaches the importance of what the authors call "perpetual unity," which means seeing the subject whole rather than bit by bit. The studio is darkened and the subject, placed in front of or on a white

25

background, is seen by students for only a second, as it is illuminated by a flashlight. During this brief look the student can only take in the over-all impression of the model; he has no opportunity to focus upon a single detail. This is certainly a sound discipline and even though a student working alone cannot conveniently practice it, the thought of it should be helpful. As Maurice Sterne said, you must draw what you have seen rather than what you see. This, of course, is a bit difficult for a beginner to grasp, but it is a goal that must eventually be reached. One way to practice it is to give yourself a very short time for the drawing, too short a time to get to the consideration of details.

Another way to accomplish the same result is through dependence upon memory. In *Composition in Landscape and Still Life* by Ernest W. Watson (Watson-Guptill Publications, 1960) the following method is proposed: "If, when driving through the countryside, you come upon an eye-stopping landscape—something you would love to paint—stop your car and sit there trying to get such a strong memory image that you can carry it back to the studio without even the benefit of a pencil notation. Don't try to memorize it in such

25   My Dog Loo, by Anna Petrovna Ostrooumova-Lebedva, Russian artist.

26   Drawing by Mervyn Peake, English. The drawing was done with ink on dampened paper. *American Artist*.

27   Charcoal-pencil drawing of cats, by Alison Marson, contemporary American, well-known for her fashion illustrations.

26

27

detail that you will be able to make a photographic reproduction of all you see: that not only would fail, it would be less interesting, if you could do it. Ask yourself first what it is that makes the scene so dramatic. Fix those big elements in mind: their shapes, their essential character and their relative importance. Don't try to remember the rest—focus only upon the essentials. You will retain nothing beyond a rough sketch. Just how big will that sycamore tree be with reference to the barn? How much foreground, how much sky? Try to see all this on your canvas. Take a good long time to record this picture on your memory film. Make it a broadly painted picture, elements massed-in simply with no detail in them.

"Now, you'll find when you get back home to your easel, even if it is not until the next day, that you can remember that picture. Render it just as you remember it, without trying to fill in details."

These are almost the words of Degas, the great French master of drawing and painting: "After all, a painting is first of all a product

28

of the artist's imagination, it ought never to be a copy. If afterwards he can add two or three natural accents, evidently that doesn't do any harm. It is much better to draw only what remains in the memory. It is a transformation during which imagination collaborates with memory; you reproduce only what strikes your eye, that is to say, the necessary . . . retaining forms and expressions. Never paint or draw immediately."

Degas further elaborated this concept. He recommended, in painting a portrait, that the model pose on the ground floor, and the artist work at his easel on the second floor; this to encourage the habit of memorizing and retaining forms.

28 Hokusai drawing, Japanese, 1760-1849. From a book *A Correspondence Course in Education*, which contains over 200 illustrations of life in old Japan. It may be news to many that teaching by correspondence is not a modern phenomenon.

29 Pen drawing of Cocks, by Evaline Ness, contemporary American.

30 Pen drawing by Boardman Robinson, American, 1876-1952.

31 Brush and ink drawing by Otis Dozier, contemporary American.

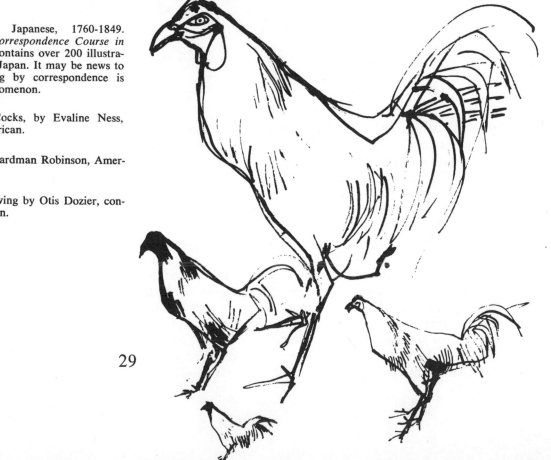

29

30

These suggestions were written for painters, but the exercises have as much value in drawing. What has been said here about the landscape is equally applicable to all types of subject matter. For example, any action drawing can come only from memory; your pet dog or cat, unless asleep, won't hold a pose for more than an instant. But by repeated observation the impression is photographed on your memory and you can reproduce it with reasonable accuracy if you have consciously tried to memorize: more often than not the need for detail will be much less than anticipated. The Chinese and Japanese are masters of the art of simplification and suggestion. It will pay to study their work often.

Simplification coexists with expression: expression is scarcely possible without simplification. When you see a friend approaching from a distance, you recognize him not by details, which you cannot see, but by the simple and well-known forms of his body and by his characteristic walk.

31

We have been putting emphasis upon expression rather than upon literal representation, but not every person who has the urge to draw *wants* to do it this way. There are some who love detail for its own sake (see [FIGURE 28] the Hokusai drawing) and to whom meticulous definition has a particular appeal. We would not discourage the ambition of anyone who delights in that kind of drawing. And, of course, detail does have its place in much expressive drawing even though it may not be the natural starting point. A drawing that has meticulous detail of observed fact may be excellent, provided that details are integrated aspects of a broadly conceived whole, and a sensitive mind has added some artistic quality to the subject, somehow so charging the picture with emotional content that it becomes a poetic response to nature and to human experience.

A reference to the work of Andrew Wyeth may help to illustrate this lyrical quality both in painting and in drawing. Wyeth paints with more than photographic reality, in a manner sometimes called "magic realism." His work, because of a mysterious quality with which he invariably endows it, reaches beyond photographic naturalism and projects a mood that comes from his inner sight rather than from the subject. The subject becomes a vehicle for a comment on life itself. No one can explain how an artist achieves such a creative result any more than it is possible to fathom his innermost nature.

If it should be asked how, in a drawing or a picture of any kind, one can achieve more than photographic reality the answer would be "Try it and find out." A drawing produced by and through search with the inner eye will often surprise even the novice.

32

Drawing by Thomas Rowlandson, English, 1756-1827. This drawing reveals either an astonishing unawareness of perspective appearance or indifference to it. The reference is to the wheels, which would afford a very rough ride at best. The diagram below is a correction. Visualized as the ends of cylinders, the wheels would properly be drawn as ellipses with their long diameters at right angles to the axis lines of the cylinders. From a structual viewpoint the carriage can be said to be resting upon two cylinders. See text for further discussion.

33

A line tracing from the painting "The Table," by André Derain, French, 1880-1954. Perspective has been violated for the purposes of design. The receding table lines diverge instead of converge.

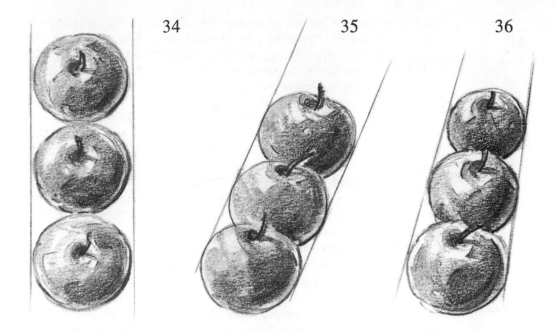

III *Perspective*

Many beginners think of perspective as a formidable and fearsome dragon and they are scared stiff at the prospect of confronting the beast. Actually the perspective dragon is a pushover. The use of but a tiny fraction of your intelligence will suffice to best him, unless, of course, the aim is to be a professional illustrator. In that case you might want to study *How to Use Creative Perspective* by Ernest W. Watson, (Reinhold Publishing Corp., 1956) which aims at the dragon's complete annihilation.

Here we tackle the subject for those who, presently, do not need to be perspective experts. A thorough knowledge of the subject is useful but there is time for that later on, when and if one feels the need of it. At the beginning it is better not to be too perspective-conscious because other things are of greater importance. Professional painters often violate perspective facts intentionally in order to give free reign to impulsive expression and, in many cases, to achieve something through design without the restriction of realistic appearance. No doubt a very talented artist is sometimes merely careless about some details of his work, as might have been the case with Thomas Rowlandson who surely knew how wheels look in such a position as seen in his drawing of the coach [FIGURE 32]. As to Figure 33 Derain's violation of perspective fact indicates his preoccupation with design rather than representation.

Let us start our perspective study with apples: three apples of equal size. In Figure 34 they are drawn as though on the floor at your feet, so that you are looking directly down at them. Seen thus, there is complete absence of perspective. Now, set the apples in a row on the table in front of you [FIGURE 35]. The nearest apple partially hides the one behind, and that one partially hides the third; and all three are drawn the same size. Do they appear to be equal in size? No; the nearest apple seems smaller than its neighbor, and the farthest one looks largest of all.

Here we are up against perspective fact No. 1. In order to make equal objects appear equal they must diminish in size as distance from the eye increases. In Figure 36 the apples have been drawn in accordance with this law. The straight lines that enclose them are not drawn parallel, they converge. If extended sufficiently the lines would meet at a point. Where is that point? For an answer refer to the simple experiment shown in Figure 37 and described in the following paragraph.

Place a picture frame with glass (at least 16 x 20 inches) so that it stands upright. Secure it in some manner to hold it in that position. It is important to have it vertical and to have the edge that rests on the table parallel with the table's edge. Set the frame so that its top edge is exactly on the level of your eyes; then take such a position that a light beam from your right eye (if you are going to squint the left one) will be just opposite the center point of the frame's top edge.

The glass represents what is termed the *picture plane* through which we look, in imagination, when viewing objects that we wish to draw. When we start to draw, the paper itself really becomes the picture plane inasmuch as the lines of our drawing follow the direction of those which might be seen through and drawn upon the glass.

Place a piece of paper, say about 6 x 9 inches, in the center of the field (the area to be included in the drawing) behind the frame as shown in the sketch [FIGURE 37]. On it place a cylindrical can. With a china marking pencil, a lithographic pencil, or any grease point that will write on glass, trace the lines of the object seen through it. The position of the eye must remain fixed during this process. When, after tracing, the lines are extended upward on the glass, they will be seen to converge and meet at a vanishing point directly opposite the eye—the center point of the frame's top edge. If the cylinder is assumed to envelop three apples, the question asked in the discussion of Figure 36 is answered. This exercise demonstrates what is known as *parallel* or *one-point perspective*. It applies to all conditions wherein receding lines are actually parallel to the direction of sight.

Next, turn the objects and the paper slightly, as in Figure 38, but do not change the position of the frame. Repeat the tracing process. The retreating lines of the long sides will now converge to a point somewhere outside and to the right of the frame. The short lines of the objects, which in Figure 37 are horizontal, now converge to a distant point at the left. If the frame were wide enough, both sets of lines would be seen to come to points on the same horizontal line—the eye-level—demonstrating *two-point perspective*. This is further shown in the drawings of the mission [FIGURE 39].

A picture frame with glass serving as the picture plane in an experiment to demonstrate the facts of one-point perspective. The outlines of objects behind the glass are traced on its surface.

37

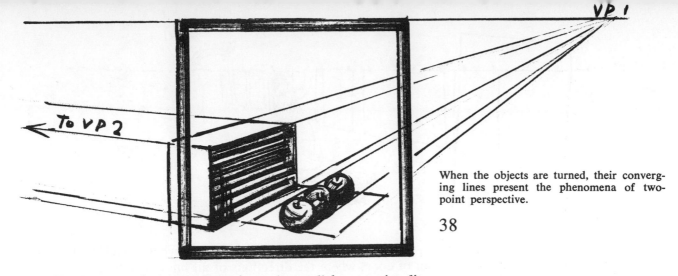

To VP2

VP 1

When the objects are turned, their converging lines present the phenomena of two-point perspective.

38

We have a rule here: all horizontal, parallel, retreating lines converge to the same point on the eye-level, which is also the horizon line. Where that point *is* depends upon the angle at which the objects are placed in relation to the picture plane. Referring again to the drawing of "The Old Mission," it is seen that the vanishing point of the lines on the greatly foreshortened face of the building—the right side—is closer to the structure than the vanishing point of the lines of the less-foreshortened side. The nearer the spectator is to the building the more acute the angle of convergence at its corner, and the closer the vanishing points. At greater distances the less acute the angle of convergence and the farther removed the vanishing points. If a tracing is made of "The Old Mission," except that the vanishing points are carried out seven or eight inches farther on both sides, the effect will be as though the spectator had gone back perhaps a hundred yards to view the structure. Should the vanishing points be extended as much as thirty inches farther, the building would be pushed into the far distance and the convergence of the lines would be scarcely noticeable. Try these experiments.

These two drawings of the Tumacacori Mission Church near Tuscon, Arizona, illustrate the relation of vanishing points to the spectator's viewpoint. In the lower sketch the spectator stands further to the left; the right side of the building is therefore more foreshortened.

39

40

How do you apply these principles when sketching buildings out of doors where the directions of all lines have to be estimated? First ascertain which of the converging lines in the building are on or near your eye-level. Hold the drawing board at arm's length, keeping it in a vertical plane with the top edge as nearly horizontal as possible. Sight along the top edge, raising or lowering the board to find a *converging* line that coincides with it. The dotted lines drawn on the photographs [FIGURES 42 and 43] indicate the spectator's eye-level. Indicate the eye-level line on your paper. Of course you will have to judge, or guess at, the correct direction of the other lines in your subject—how much they slant up or down in relation to the eye-level—but knowledge of the principle of convergence will enable you to approximate their direction. You can check up on a diagrammatic analysis (a tracing overlay) when you return home. Eventually you will become expert enough simply to draw what you see without thinking very much about diagrams.

Suppose the street you are drawing, instead of being level, is at an incline, either up or down. The diagrams in Figure 41 illustrate the perspective facts of a downhill street. The street, in our model, is a cardboard plane, raised in the foreground (b) to give it a rather steep descent. When the street is level (a), its lines are parallel with those of the building and converge with them to a vanishing point on the horizon line (the eye-level). But when tilted (b) they meet at a point directly below the vanishing point of the building lines in a line known as the *vanishing trace,* its distance below the eye-level depending upon the slant of the street.

Cardboard models may be used to visualize the perspective facts of an inclined street.

41

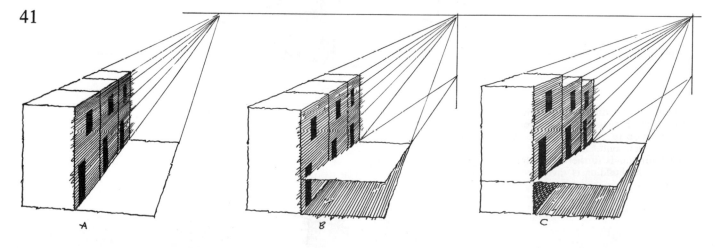

A   B   C

42

The facts of one-point perspective are shown superimposed on this photograph of a street in Cheddar, England. The horizontal dotted line represents the eye-level (in this case the level of the camera lens).

43

Photographs of a barn on an inclined road. The upper picture was taken from below; the lower photograph from above, looking down hill.

The important fact to remember is that the tipping of the street plane *does not affect the perspective of the building lines;* an obvious enough truth, yet a frequent point of confusion for beginners.

In order to reproduce the true effect of a street on such an incline, the heights of the three house-units in our model have been adjusted (c) at intervals to conform to the circumstances.

In Figure 43 are photographs of a barn on an inclined road. One picture was made from below, another from above. So in the former the eye-level (dotted line) is low on the building. In the latter it is higher, coinciding with the clapboards which, in the print, are horizontal at that point. The vanishing points of the building's short lines are at too great a distance to permit showing them on the page.

The drawing of a street in an English hill town [FIGURE 44] illustrates the perspective facts when the spectator is standing in the street looking up. In such a situation there are two vanishing points as demonstrated in the accompanying line analysis. The horizontal building lines always converge to the same point at the eye-level (dotted line). The street lines here converge to a higher point because we are looking up the hill. The inclination of the street will be most evident in a drawing when horizontal building lines are given as much emphasis as possible in order to contrast with the inclined street lines.

The perspective facts involved in drawing interiors are similar to those already demonstrated in exterior subjects. The principal difference being in the observer's position: in one case he is outside, in the other, inside. In Figure 46 we see that the converging lines of all foreshortened surfaces—walls, floors, ceiling, rug and any furniture that may line up with the side walls—meet at O, a point on the level of the observer's eye, in the center of the rear wall; the assumption being that the spectator stands in the center of the room and directs his gaze in the general direction of O. Hence the room's corners, X and Y, are equidistant from him and should appear of equal height. The rear wall, therefore, should be represented as a perfect rectangle.

In Figure 47 the spectator has moved to the left side of the room; therefore, assuming that he directs his gaze parallel with the receding walls, the vanishing point moves to the left, as shown. However, if he directs his eyes in the general area of the Y corner we have to make a new diagram to represent the changed viewpoint. The Y corner, being farthest from him, would appear perspectively shorter than the X corner, thus creating an effect, theoretically, like that of Figure 48, in which the lines of the side walls converge, as in Figure 47, but those of the rear wall and all objects parallel with it (the rug) converge as shown. This gives what may appropriately be termed *bastard* two-point perspective, being contrary to the way the room actually looks to the eye of a person in the described circumstances. It does represent the way the room would be seen by the camera's lens, which often differs radically from the

44

Pencil drawing made in an English village. It demonstrates the perspective facts observed when buildings border an inclined street. The line diagram analysis shows this to be an example of *two-point* perspective.

human eye. The person taking the position described in Figure 48, and looking slightly toward the Y corner would see the left wall but dimly in the periphery of his vision. This conclusion can readily be proved by experiment. Figure 49 represents what might be called normal appearance, the left wall not being seen at all.

When the direction of sight aims directly at the corner, as in Figure 50, there is equal foreshortening and convergence of both walls. This is the viewpoint in the sketch of the room interior [FIGURE 45].

Although, as previously stated, the appearance of a room represented by the diagram in Figure 48 is contrary to normal vision, it is one that has practical value inasmuch as it is more inclusive than Figure 49. It is commonly used by architects and interior decorators for obvious reasons. In this kind of treatment there can be distorted effects when too much of the room's depth is included as in Figure 48, where the rug, brought into the near foreground, takes on an unnaturally acute angle. However, in this day of close-up photography we have become used to all kinds of distortions which formerly were not tolerated.

When sketching interiors it is advisable first to ascertain the height of the eye-level. The chances are that in your subject there will be some horizontal lines of both side walls that are on your eye-level; that is, they actually will be horizontal in your drawing. In the pencil sketch [FIGURE 45] the eye-level is the bottom edge of the picture behind the lamp. The suggestion for sighting along the top edge of your drawing board can be applied profitably here.

45

Pencil sketch of the corner of a living room. Drawn from the point of view shown in Figure 50.

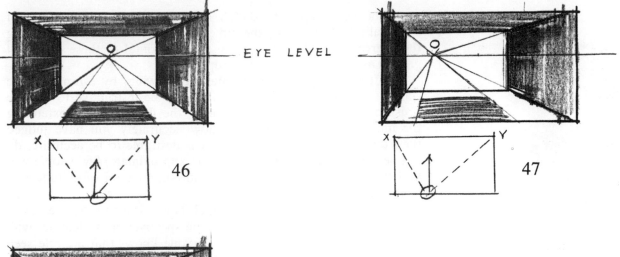

EYE LEVEL

46

X Y

47

X Y

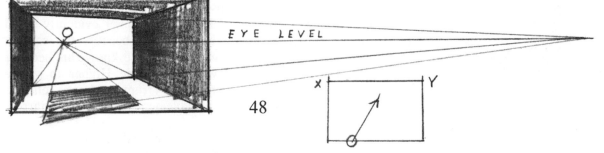

EYE LEVEL

48

X Y

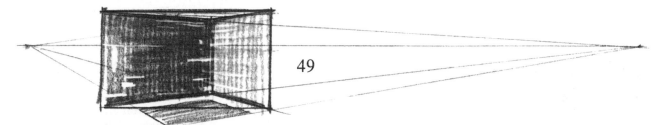

49

X Y

50

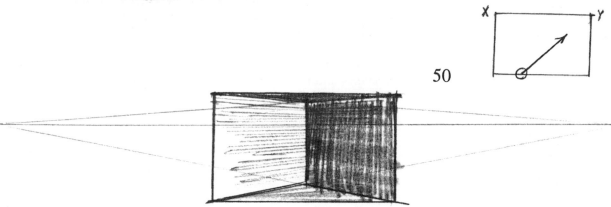

The next step is to sketch in the ceiling and floor lines of both walls. Sighting along the top edge of your board and estimating the degree of the deflection from the horizontal of these lines will greatly assist in placing them properly.

After having made your interior drawing, by estimating the slant of the lines as best you can, it will be instructive to lay the finished drawing on a large table or the floor and, by extending the lines of each wall, discover how accurately you have judged their directions. However, though it is desirable to be accurate, do not be concerned if your guess is only approximate; few people will be conscious of slight errors. More important than exactitude is a free, spirited impression.

The photograph of the Sentinel Tower [FIGURE 51] serves to demonstrate one of the essential perspective facts dealing with cylindrical and circular objects. Everyone knows that a circle seen in perspective appears as an ellipse. When held horizontally at eye-level it is merely a straight line. The photographer evidently stood upon something slightly above the pavement because the camera was on a level with the top of the doorway. We know this because the stone courses at that level show a straight line. Higher up we see the masonry joints forming ever wider (front to back) ellipses toward the top of the tower; at the pavement level, a very narrow ellipse.

What is an ellipse? It is a symmetrical, geometric figure [FIGURE 52], not an oval. When folded on either the long or short diameter, each folded half lies exactly on its corresponding half. That is not a perfect geometric definition. The dictionary is more specific. However the practical way to acquire the correct concept of an ellipse is to make many tracings of ellipses from photographs. The camera gives correct perspective results in this case, although it does not tell the truth in many other situations.

In practicing ellipses, use a free arm movement. It is almost impossible to draw a good ellipse with finger movement.

The table service sketch [FIGURE 54] presents a situation that is commonly encountered—a combination of circular and rectangular shapes. This is an important relationship that the student should try to master as soon as possible by persistent practice drawing of arrangements similar to this one. A common error is to draw the circular shapes and rectangular shapes as though each were seen from a different eye-level.

51 Sentinel Tower of Fort Castillo de Marcos in St. Augustine, Florida.

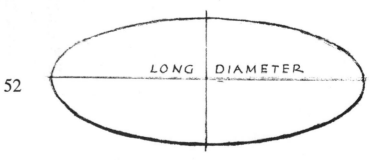

52

LONG DIAMETER

Another important perspective fact is demonstrated in Figure 53. The long diameter of the ellipse always appears at right angles to the axis of a cylinder whatever the cylinder's position. Thus, when the cylinder is lying on its side, the long diameter of the elliptical end is not a vertical line, but is slanted at a 45-degree angle to the cylinder's axis as shown. This can be puzzling at first because the long diameter of the ellipse may be confused with a structural line on the circle's face such as a line through the numerals VI and XII on a clock face. In a circle, that structural line is always vertical while the axis of the ellipse is a variable, according to the observer's

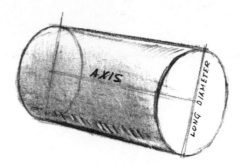

53

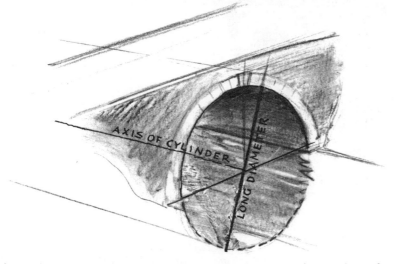

viewpoint—the axis of the ellipse being an imaginary line of perspective appearance. In this connection refer again to Figure 32, the drawing by Thomas Rowlandson and the diagram underneath it. Note that (in the diagram) the wheels are visualized as the ends of cylinders and that the ellipses which represent them in perspective are constructed on long diameters which are at right angles to the axes lines of the cylinders. It is usually helpful when drawing circles in perspective to visualize them as the ends of imaginary cylinders. Thus the arch of the bridge can be thought of as lying upon a huge cylinder.

54

55   Pen drawing by Herbert Railton, English.

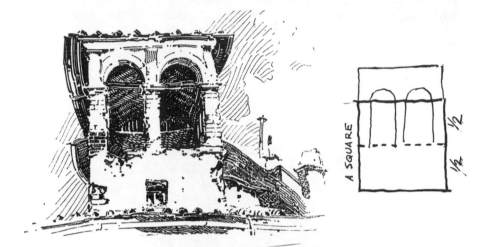

58   59

56

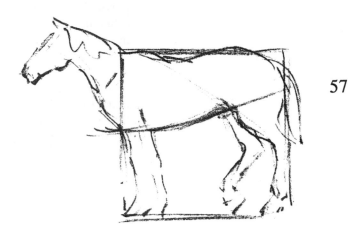

57

IV *Measurement and Form Analysis*

All representational drawing implies measurement of some kind. We cannot indicate the character of any object without stating its correct proportion and the relationship of all parts to the whole. The mechanical draftsman can lay a ruler on his drawings, measuring in inches and feet, but in freehand drawing this, of course, is impossible. Proportion takes the place of linear measurement even when, as in the tower and the door [FIGURES 55 and 56] there is no perspective problem. The artist does not need to know the dimensions of objects in feet or inches; he is concerned only with the relation of width to height. A crude way of judging proportion is by pencil measurement, sighting along a pencil held at arm's length. Although this method is not wholly impractical, it is far from accurate because it is next to impossible to hold a pencil exactly at right angles to the direction of sight, as though it were placed against an imaginary windowpane through which one might be looking. The slightest deviation of the measuring pencil from this position flat against the picture plane renders measurements almost useless.

How then can we deal with proportion? If we have a true concept of a square and, in imagination, view our subject in relation to it, we have a dependable method of measurement. We note, for example, that the door [FIGURE 56] occupies practically two squares, though not quite. The diagram accompanying Railton's bell tower [FIGURE 55] shows that our square includes the lower part up to the springing of the arches. The sills of the windows rest in a bisecting line, and the upper portion is a little less than a half square.

While the square might seem the last shape to be associated with a horse [FIGURE 57], it does tell something important about this particular horse. However, the square may not serve similarly for other horses since there is as great variation in animal structure as in the human form.

Every professional artist measures objects in this way consciously or subconsciously; there really is no other way. The only problem is the acquisition of a true concept of the square; one must learn this so thoroughly that its use is no problem at all. The way to do this is to draw innumerable squares freehand, hundreds perhaps, testing each with a ruler, until you are sure of yourself. In addition, measure many objects in photographs by the use of tracing overlays.

61

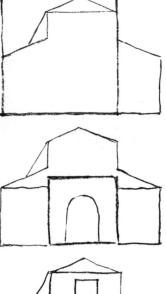

60

When you plan to sketch outdoors take along a transparent plastic film upon which you have drawn a two-inch square. Squinting one eye, study the subject through it. At length you will be able to dispense even with this aid, though you should not be ashamed to use it. If your square has bisecting lines these will help to locate some important structural divisions in the object, as shown in the photograph of the Tumacacori Mission [FIGURE 59].

As one becomes accustomed to using the square in sketching, its application will become almost automatic. The sketch and diagrams of a Romanesque church [FIGURE 60] demonstrate how very useful this kind of measurement can be in drawing a rather complicated subject.

The sketch in Figure 58 is a demonstration of a different use of the square: the square in *perspective*. This admits of no mechanical help; all depends upon the practiced eye of the artist who knows what a square looks like when viewed from all angles and in foreshortened positions. This means acquiring a true concept of the

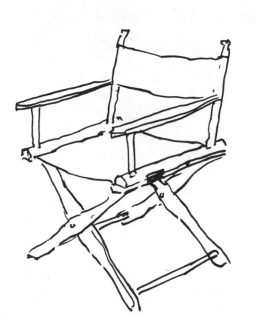

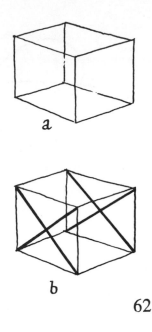

a

b

62

c

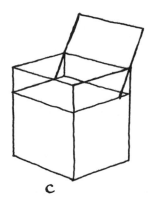

63

64

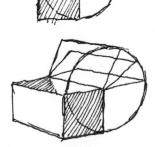

cube so that it can be used as a unit of measure as is the square. The best way to acquire this skill is to practice drawing cubes in all possible positions until you are positive of your judgment. You should be warned that this will take a lot of practice, but the result is well worth the effort. The perspective square is far more useful than the geometric square because you usually view your subject when its faces are foreshortened, turned away from you. The enclosing geometric square can, of course, be combined with the perspective square when used first to enclose measurements of the whole form as shown in the diagram [FIGURE 58].

The idea of measurement leads naturally to the analysis of objects based on geometric forms to which they can be related. A simple example is Figure 62, the folding camp chair. We envision the seat and legs section as a rectangular solid (a). Diagonal lines are drawn on opposite ends (b). On top of the seat box we sketch a shallow box (c) which locates the arms. The slant of the chairback is a simple matter. Without this kind of analysis the crossed legs might well be touching the floor at impossible points.

The importance of form analysis is well demonstrated by the failure of Thomas Rowlandson's drawing of the coach [CHAPTER III, FIGURE 32]. The diagram accompanying it shows how different his result would have been if he had conceived of the coach body as resting upon two cylinders.

The drawing of such a simple object as the scotch tape holder [FIGURE 63] involves the same kind of analytical thinking. Similarly the hinged lid of a box [FIGURE 64] can easily be drawn with accuracy when its movement in opening is related to the radii of a circle.

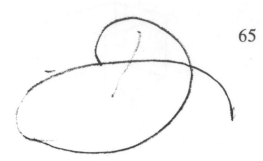

65

Sketches by Warren Baumgartner, contemporary American.

a

66

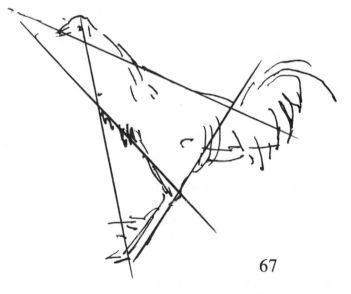

b

c

67

Analysis of the drawing of Cocks, by Evaline Ness, reproduced in Chapter II, Figure 29.

d

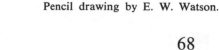
Pencil drawing by E. W. Watson.

68

69

70

Form analysis may involve the sphere, the half-sphere (dome), pyramid, cone, and triangle. Note how the triangle has served in analysis of the tree [FIGURE 68], and the drawing of the cock, by Evaline Ness [FIGURE 67].

By envisioning enclosing shapes for any kind of free form such as Van Gogh's drawing of the peasant woman [FIGURE 69], we assure ourselves of correct over-all proportion at the outset. If we then analyze the structure of dominant action by striking lines across the form we have a usable pattern for the development of the figure. Refer also to the analysis of trees in Chapter XVI. Baumgartner's drawings of dogs [FIGURES 65 and 66] can be profitably analysed as shown in the diagrams that accompany them. Note how in Figure 66 (c) a bisecting line struck across the elliptical outline locates the action of the hind leg; and in (d) the shoulder line makes an acute angle with it.

Another kind of analysis is illustrated in Figure 70. Here the dark ribbon of movement is the key to the entire action of the figure of the prizefighter.

Although this chapter touches only fundamentally upon measurement and analysis, the student may become alert to the necessity of this kind of structural thinking in all his drawing experience.

Analysis of the drawing of a prizefighter by Mahonri Young, reproduced in Chapter I, Figure 9.

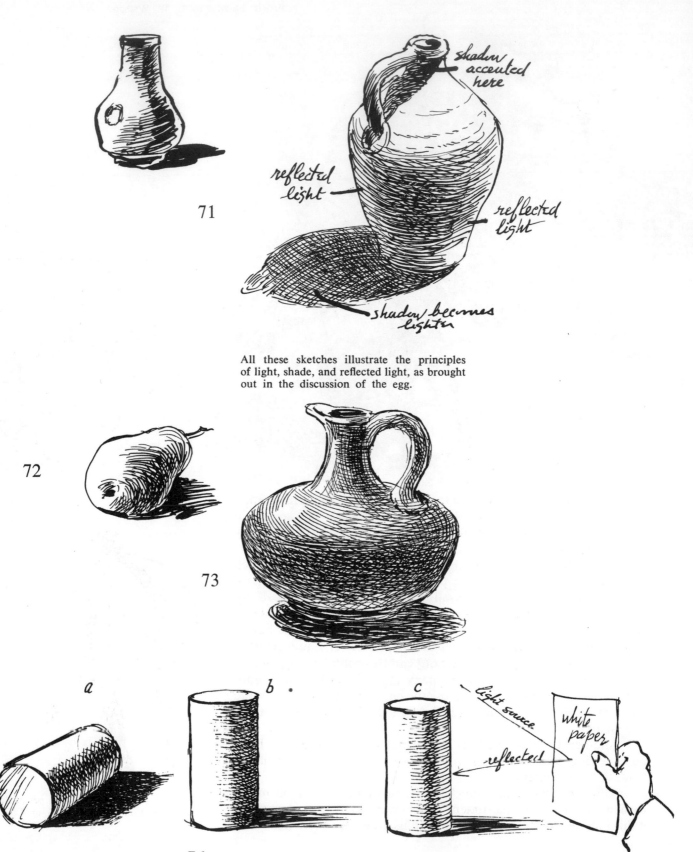

71

shadow
accented
here

reflected
light

reflected
light

shadow becomes
lighter

All these sketches illustrate the principles
of light, shade, and reflected light, as brought
out in the discussion of the egg.

72

73

a

b

c

light source

white
paper

reflected

76

74 Head of a Girl, by Jean Baptiste Greuze, French, 1725-1805. The Metropolitan Museum of Art.

V *Light, Shade, and Shadow*

Since in nature all form is so largely defined by light, shade, and shadow this phenomenon is something that invites considerable study. Color is a definite factor also, but to a lesser extent; it can reasonably be ignored in our present study.

Shade is the absence, on objects, of direct light. *Shadow* is the obstruction of light by intervening objects. *Reflected light* is light that is thrown from adjacent illuminated areas into shaded surfaces. *High light* is a mirror-like reflection of the light source upon high points of the object's lighted areas; it occurs only on highly polished surfaces.

These essential facts are dramatically demonstrated by placing an egg in strong light on a white ground. What you see may surprise you: the cast shadow will be darker than expected; the shaded side of the egg will be darkest where indicated in the diagram [FIGURE 75]. The reflected light may appear to be nearly as light as the illuminated area. This is due to its contrast with the dark shadow. The high light will appear as indicated. But rather than accept the author's word, you should observe these facts of light for yourself.

Place the egg on a piece of gray paper or fabric; then on a jet-black ground. Note that the darker the ground, the weaker the reflected light. On a black ground there will be no reflection.

Experiment with a cylinder [FIGURE 76]. Wrap a piece of paper around any cylindrical can. Lay it on its side (a), and observe the light phenomena similar to those demonstrated with the egg. There will be no high light unless the cylinder has a polished surface, in

75

77

78

79

80

81

which case it may be a thin line of brilliance running along the lighted area of the cylinder's length.

Stand the cylinder on its end [FIGURE 76b], again on white paper. The reflected light is missing until a sheet of paper is held near it, as in (c). Then the darkest part of the cylinder will be seen to be inside its shaded contour instead of on the extreme edge. Try the same experiment with a cone.

These experiments demonstrate phenomena that are applicable to the rendering of all spherical, conical and cylindrical objects. Reflected light is often exaggerated in order to force the third-dimensional effect. Even when in nature there is no noticeable reflected light, as is the case in a round tower standing alone [FIGURES 77 and 78], the artist usually will take advantage of this phenomenon to give completeness to its cylindrical appearance. When such a tower is related to a wall, as in Figure 79, the reflected light is very obvious.

Reflections upon plane surfaces are of equal illustrative value as is demonstrated in Figure 80 where the illuminated façade of the square building throws its light back into the shadow on the tower.

In dark tree trunks and branches reflected light is practically nonexistent, but in employing it in his drawings the artist enhances the appearance of roundness [FIGURE 81].

Much can be learned by the student through his own observations and through experiments similar to some made in a series of drawings commissioned by a pencil company as advertisements to demonstrate the exceptional capacity of the pencil for recording various light effects. The assignment was unique and rewarding. For me it was a search for, and a discovery of, the beauty and drama revealed by strong light focused upon arrangements of simple paper models. The models, cut and shaped from stiff white paper, were set up on a shadow box which excluded all light except that from a 150-watt floor lamp which could be raised, lowered and turned in all directions and focused upon the setup. With the changing direction of light, shadows took on the greatest variety of dramatic effects, the most interesting of which was rendered meticulously in pencil and reproduced in a full-page advertisement. One of these compositions [FIGURE 83] is reproduced here at greatly reduced size merely to show the kind of setup described; at this reduction it does not reproduce the subtle effects of the pencil technique.

82

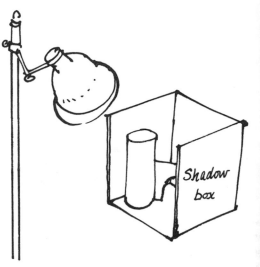

Shadow box

83

One of a series of light and shade studies, prepared as advertisements for a pencil company by Ernest W. Watson. The models were made from white bristol board, and provided a wide range of lighting effects.

The project is described here because it offers a fascinating method for study of intriguing light effects. Some of the models can be patterned after simple architectural forms such as arches, fountains, round towers, stairs, etc. Abstract elements as simple as those indicated [FIGURE 82] do as well for purposes of demonstration but it may be more fun to simulate some recognizable subject. However, it is better not to become too involved with representation. If the models are set up on a cardboard which can be revolved, the great variety of changing patterns will appear exciting. Even if you should not want to draw the models—though this certainly is advisable— the experience of creating them and observing the drama of light effects is in itself most instructive. If you are an amateur photographer it might be interesting to photograph your setups.

a

HB

2B

5B

b

c

d

e

f

g

h

85

VI *Pencil*

The pencil is quite likely to be the first tool to suggest itself to the amateur draftsman because it is familiar to everyone, even though it may have been used only for writing shopping lists. Its utter simplicity invites a beginner who may not want to equip himself with other art materials until he has tried himself out with a tool he knows at least something about.

If the student has not done considerable experimenting with the pencil he will be surprised to learn how versatile it is and how effective a means of art expression.

There are many name brands of graphite pencils. Although some are no doubt better than others, all give about the same result. What matters is the manner in which they are used. The harder leads, say HB, F, H and 2H, are most useful for sharp line work; the B grades, being of softer graphite, do not hold a point so well and are naturally adapted for bolder lines or brush-like tones. Hard leads are most useful for small-scale drawing; softer leads are less limited in the matter of size, but even the softest give better results in relatively small drawings. A drawing over 8 x 10 inches begins to tax the resources of any pencil, although some artists certainly work effectively at much larger scale. However, other media, such as charcoal, the brush, and the felt nib are more at home in large-scale work.

Take a 3B or a 4B pencil and sharpen it to a fairly sharp point with a knife. (The mechanical character of a point made by a sharpener is anathema to the author.) On a piece of drawing paper that

86

Carbon pencil sketch by Norman Kent. The original is twice the size of this reproduction.

has some tooth—not too smooth, that is—make the test suggested in Figure 84a, all the while keeping the pencil from turning. As the lead wears down, the stroke becomes increasingly wider until it reaches the maximum diameter of the lead; the point will then look as shown in Figure 84c. This is not a chisel edge, that is, one that has been sharpened on both sides to a sharp edge, in contrast to the worn-down character produced by this exercise.

Now, working with this worn-down point on a paper like Alexis (Strathmore) or Aquabee Drawing 812 (Bee Paper Co.), both good pencil papers that are available in most stores, it will be discovered that the lighter tones—those necessarily produced by lighter pressure of a soft lead—have a grained quality due to the lead skimming rather lightly over the roughness of the paper's surface. If one does not object to this grained technique—there are times when it is most effective—a single soft pencil suffices for the entire rendering of the drawing.

However, the broad-stroke technique offers a distinctive charm that is characteristic of the pencil. In this manner of working all strokes, light as well as dark, have the smooth, crisp quality that

87

Sketch of a street in Rockport, Massachusetts, by Theodore Kautsky, American, 1896-1953. Reproduced at one-half size of the original. Kautsky used a very soft graphite pencil with an extra thick lead.

results from bearing down and "ironing-out" the paper's surface. For lighter tones use harder leads with considerable pressure. This method is illustrated in Figure 84b [see also FIGURE 85], where three pencils, hard, medium and soft, were used. It is not unusual to see an artist working with a handful of pencils of many different grades, expertly selecting just the right lead to suit the tonal area being rendered. Like a beginner on the typewriter learning how to strike the right keys, the student of broad-stroke may at first find some awkwardness with his battery of pencils; yet with a little practice the technique will become second nature.

What we have been saying about the use of several degrees of lead refers to work on papers that have some tooth, or roughness. On a smoother paper you can manage with one or two pencils, though not all smooth surfaces will yield satisfying results; some papers are so hard and smooth—primarily designed for pen drawing—that they are very unsympathetic to the pencil. One of the best smooth papers for the pencil is Aquabee Satin Finish, which is quite generally available. On this surface a single soft lead will satisfactorily render smooth tones in a wide range of values. This might be a 4B, 5B or 6B according to atmospheric conditions; when there is much humidity the paper becomes damp and softer leads are needed. A rather expensive and altogether delightful paper that makes broad-stroke possible with but one or two leads—these in the harder range—is Video. It is available in New York and probably elsewhere. This is a clay-coated paper, a surface that not only yields beautiful tones but permits scraping-out of white lines and small areas of white within pencil tones by the use of a sharp edge or point. A razor blade is ideal.

Finding the right paper is of greatest importance and this can be done only by experimentation. The beginner usually does not appreciate this and he may continue working on an unsympathetic surface with disappointing results. Explore papers in your art supply store; buy different papers and experiment with them.

Another essential factor in pencil work should be emphasized. This is the practice of having several sheets of paper under the drawing to provide a yielding surface into which the lead can bite. Remember also to keep the pencil from turning in the fingers when working in broad-stroke. Often however the artist may want to turn the lead in broad-stroke, as shown in Figure 84d, in order to render some sharp thin lines to serve as accents here and there.

What has been said up to now applies to broad-stroke technique with graphite or "lead" pencils. The Wolff pencil leads are quite different and not as sympathetic to some artists (more so to others). This pencil does have one distinct advantage: its complete absence of shine makes it somewhat more practical for drawings that are to be reproduced on the printing press.

Broad-stroke is only one way of using pencils. Much can be done in what can be called the scumbling method. In this technique there is no effort to produce firm, wide strokes; the pencil is employed in much the same manner as charcoal or crayon, one soft pencil usually sufficing for the work. The pencil often is held as are charcoal sticks, the flat side of the lead doing the work [FIGURE 84e] with the pencil held in the palm of the hand.

Harder lead pencils are often used more like the pen [see Sadolin's pen drawing, CHAPTER VIII, FIGURE 114] rendering the sketch throughout in sharp thin lines.

The tortillon stump [FIGURE 84f] is a useful adjunct to the pencil. It is a rolled paper cylinder, somewhat pointed on the business end. Gently rubbed over the pencil strokes it produces a very smooth tone as seen in Figures 84f and g. The stump should be used with great caution; if too generally employed it gives the sketch a soft, characterless quality. But a touch of the stump here and there serves to add pleasant technical variety to pencil drawing.

The kneaded rubber [FIGURE 84h] is an indispensable tool, not so much for erasing (although it is needed for that too) as for playing a creative part in the rendering. Unlike most erasers it "lifts" the pencil tones without smearing them. Kneaded rubbers come in rectangular blocks. Cut or tear off a piece the size of the end of your thumb and knead it between thumb and fingers until it becomes soft

Hard
Leads

Medium

Very
Soft

Medium

Very
soft

Saint Ives, Cornwall

and pliable. When it is in this condition, a tone can be lightened merely by pressing the rubber down upon it and lifting it up without rubbing. In using it as a drawing tool pinch it to a sharp edge. With gentle rubbing, it can then strike into tones as in Figure 84g, at the arrow. This is an extremely useful collaborative adjunct to the pencil.

The charcoal pencil should also be mentioned. This is hard charcoal compressed into pencil form. It is not adapted to broad-stroke technique, being more closely related in handling to charcoal than to either graphite or carbon pencils. It can be sharpened on a sandpaper pad to a good point. It is often used to add line emphasis to wash drawings.

Many artists make much use of the lithographic pencil, a greasy lead which has qualities that will soon be discovered through experimentation. It reproduces very well because it has no shine.

There are many pencil drawings in this book which should be consulted in addition to those included in the present chapter.

88

St. Ives, Cornwall, England, by E. W. Watson. This sketch illustrates the use of hard, medium, and soft leads on a paper having a slight tooth.

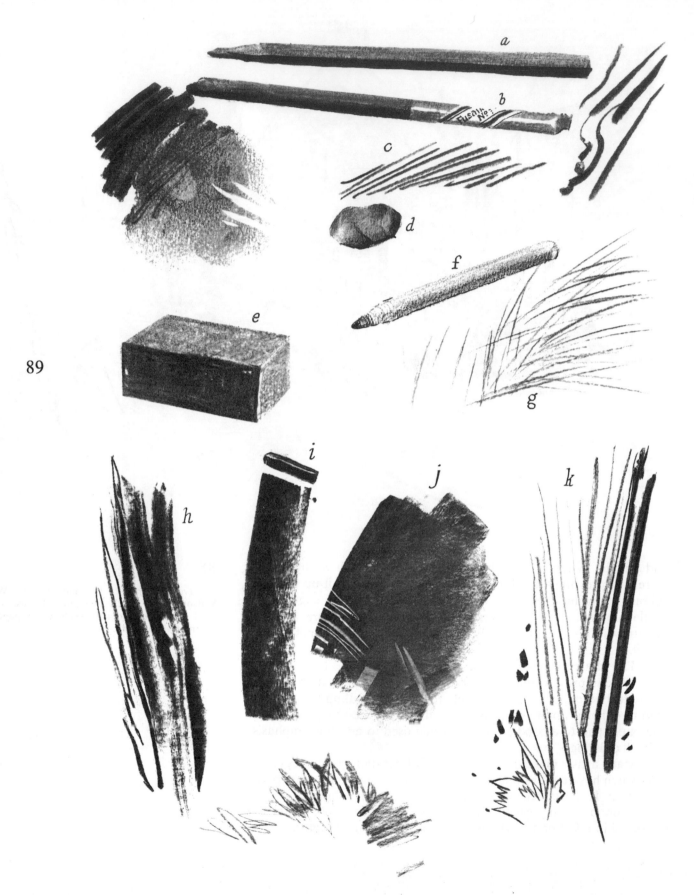

90

VII *Charcoal*

Charcoal is one of the most flexible and most expressive of all black-and-white mediums. Soft charcoal (vine charcoal) comes in round sticks [FIGURE 89b]. It will produce broad masses of tone quickly and easily. When rubbed with the thumb it spreads out into a variety of velvet-like tones from black to very light gray.

Harder, flat-sided sticks [FIGURE 89a] are useful for more meticulous light-toned work and for lines such as seen in Figures 89c and g. They can be pointed on a sandpaper pad for detail treatments. Both hard and soft charcoal can be combined in the same drawing: soft sticks for masses, hard sticks for details and more delicate work. Hard charcoal for some reason seems to be difficult to find in art supply stores, but the soft variety can be used effectively in almost all situations.

The stump [FIGURE 89f] can be used for rubbing the charcoal in delicate modeling but one should use it sparingly and avoid losing the freshness of the medium. The rectangular sponge-rubber [FIGURE 89e] is sometimes useful in spreading large masses of soft charcoal, but it can be dispensed with; the thumb is usually better.

Kneaded rubber is almost as essential as the charcoal itself. It really is more of a drawing tool than an eraser. It comes in small rectangular cakes wrapped in cellophane. A small piece is broken off [FIGURE 89d] and kneaded between the thumb and forefinger until, becoming warm, it is soft and pliable. In cold weather lay it on a radiator to soften it. The rubber has to be continuously kneaded so that it always presents a clean surface as its use continues. Pinched

91

Charcoal pencil drawing by E. W. Watson, same size as the original. Tuscon, Arizona.

to a point or to an edge, it will lift or pick out white shapes or accents from tonal masses, as seen in Figure 89b.

The demonstrations on the lower half of the page were made with soft sticks. In Figure 89i, a broken piece less than an inch wide was drawn down on the paper with the charcoal lying flat, as pictured. Short lengths also produced Figure 89j. Figure 89h, which suggests leaves or stalks, was made with a soft stick held between thumb and forefinger and lying in the palm of the hand, in this position being nearly parallel with paper. The marks in Figure 89k were made with a soft stick. They show how versatile this very soft charcoal is. The thin strokes were produced with the unsharpened end of the stick. Soft charcoal is very brittle which means it has to be held rather close to the drawing edge. For this reason artists usually work with the short, broken lengths.

92   Woman Cleaning A Cauldron, by Vincent
van Gogh, Dutch, 1853-1890. Charcoal
drawing on paper, 24 inches high. Albright
Art Gallery, Buffalo, New York.

93

The charcoal pencil is quite a different medium and a useful one. It has an additive that hardens the charcoal so that it holds a point and can be used for delineation that is not possible with the sticks. It can be a supplement to the sticks, adding sharp line technique to massed technique. The saguaro trees and the yucca [FIGURE 91] were sketched with the charcoal pencil.

The quality of paper employed in charcoal drawing is of utmost importance. Smooth papers will not do; those having considerable tooth are necessary. "Charcoal paper" is generally used in figure and portrait drawing in schools, but it is by no means the best all around surface. Illustration and bristol boards are both pleasantly receptive. The drawing by S. Csoka [FIGURE 94] was made on watercolor paper, as was the portrait of Roy Mason [CHAPTER XIII, FIGURE 186]. There are other papers which the student might try. It is ad-

94　Charcoal on watercolor paper. S. Csoka, contemporary American.

93

Still life, charcoal on illustration board, by E. W. Watson. One-half size of the original. Still life studies afford excellent opportunity for exploring the medium as well as searching for esthetic values. See the analytical study of this same subject done with felt tip (Chapter XII, Figure 168). Such simple analyses help define the subject's basic structure.

95

Charcoal figure sketch by Marshall Davis, contemporary American. Here the intent is quite the opposite of the Csoka study. Subtle tonality and suggestion contrast with the direct line attack of the Csoka drawing. The soft charcoal has been rubbed with the fingers.

visable in taking up any medium to do a lot of experimenting on various papers in order to discover their possibilities. Beginners are likely to do less of it than they should.

In the drawing by Henry C. Pitz [FIGURE 96], soft charcoal has been skillfully combined with pen and wash to achieve a unique effect. Charcoal, as an adjunct to various line mediums, supplies tone and mass quickly, and is very flexible. Graphite pencils, however, are incompatible with charcoal.

Because charcoal affords such diversity of treatment it is a favorite with artists both for on-the-spot sketching, and for studies made in the studio. Before getting used to handling charcoal

96

Charcoal drawing by Henry C. Pitz, contemporary American. From *Drawing Trees*, by Henry C. Pitz, Watson-Guptill Publications, Inc.

it appears to be a messy medium but one soon learns to control it efficiently. All charcoal drawings should be "fixed," by spraying with one of the modern plastic sprays.

The cats by Alison [CHAPTER II, FIGURE 27] were done with a 2B charcoal pencil—she prefers a brand named *Charco*, made by the Eagle Pencil Company. She draws on layout paper, often using the side of the lead as well as the point.

The Belleroche drawing [CHAPTER XIII, FIGURE 187] is a lithograph but the technique closely resembles charcoal when the stone upon which the lithograph is drawn has a roughly grained surface.

97   Pen and ink drawing by Walter Jack Duncan, who was one of America's "old masters" of illustration. Before the day of halftone reproduction his work was in much demand by editors and publishers. His drawing of the old shipyard is as fine a landscape as he ever did. Rendered with a fine pen, it combines tonal masses with beautiful line work. The original is slightly larger than this reproduction. *American Artist* magazine.

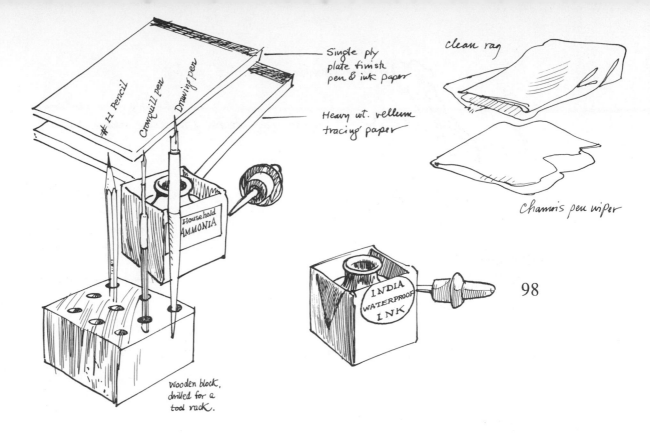

Single ply
plate finish
pen & ink paper

Heavy wt. vellum
tracing paper

clean rag

Chamois pen wiper

H Pencil

Crowquill pen

Drawing pen

Household
AMMONIA

INDIA
WATERPROOF
INK

98

Wooden block,
drilled for a
tool rack.

VIII   *Pen and Ink*

Pen and ink is one of the most ancient of drawing mediums. Long before the invention of our steel pens, artists were drawing with sticks dipped in some kind of ink. From the reed, a hollow stalk that grows in marshy land, very serviceable pens were made by shaping with the knife. Quills from turkeys and other large birds also became widely used in drawing, and in writing as well. All of these pens are still valued by contemporary artists because of properties not found in pens made of steel, however versatile these may be. Directions for making reed and quill pens are given later in this chapter.

As a direct extension of the hand and fingers, the pen is completely autographic; it instantly transmits to paper every impulse of the hand. Its use encompasses the full range of drawing, from the fleeting sketch to the most complex symphony of detail and tonal effect, such as is seen in the Walter Jack Duncan drawing [FIGURE 97]. It is a positive medium: whatever is set down has to remain, erasure is practically out of the question. So the pen draftsman must acquire a fearless attitude; timid, tentative lines are entirely out of character. This should frighten no one because with persistence the student very soon feels at home with the medium.

Study of all the pen drawings reproduced in this book will reveal the infinite possibilities of the pen as a medium of expression. While the student is making his own experiments, these examples should be carefully examined.

Very simple equipment is sufficient. One needs only two or

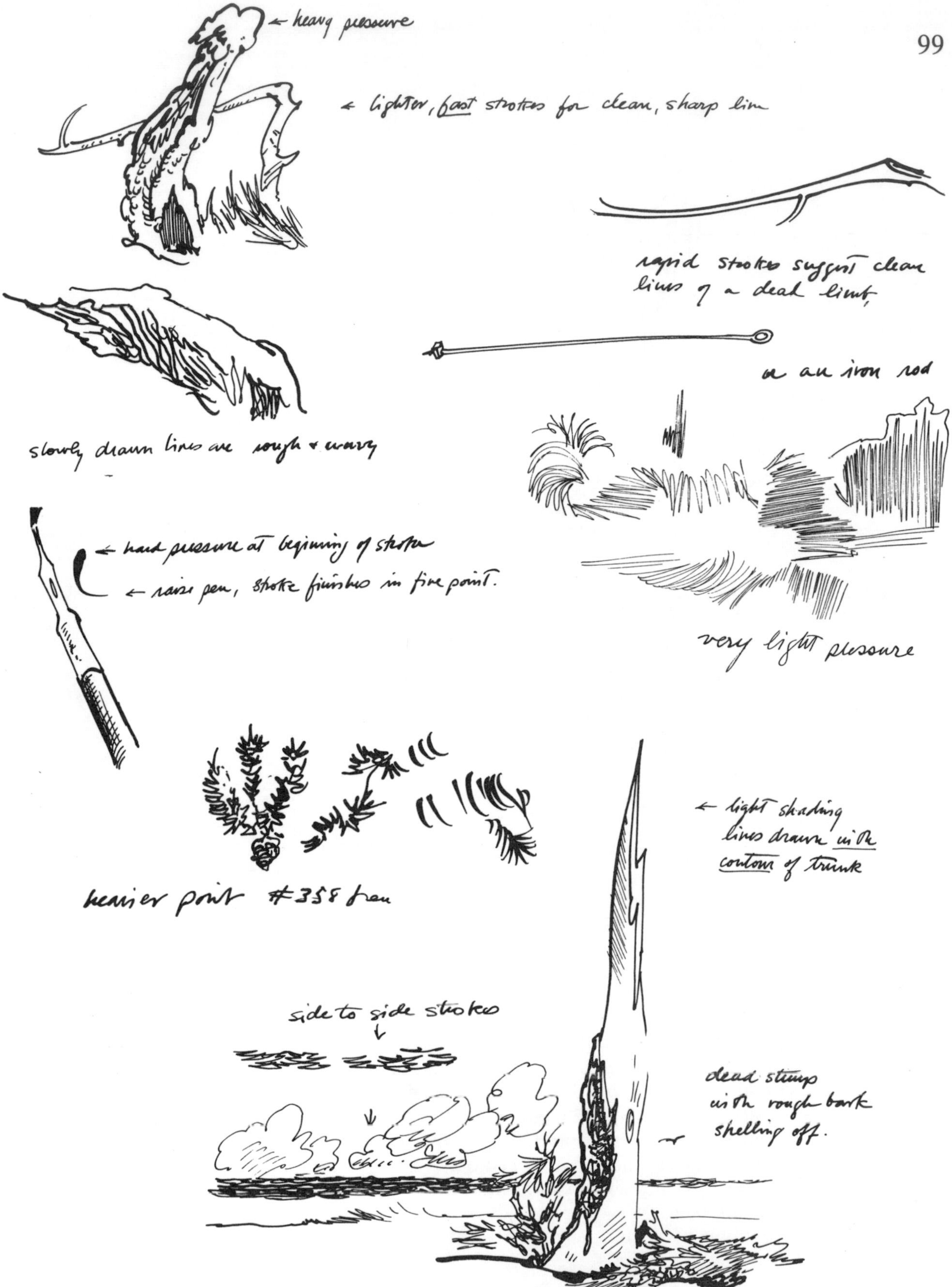

← heavy pressure

← lighter, _fast_ strokes for clean, sharp line

rapid strokes suggest clean
lines of a dead limb

slowly drawn lines are rough & wavy

or an iron rod

← hard pressure at beginning of stroke
← raise pen, stroke finishes in fine point.

very light pressure

heavier point #358 pen

← light shading
lines drawn with
contour of trunk

side to side strokes

dead stump
with rough bark
shelling off.

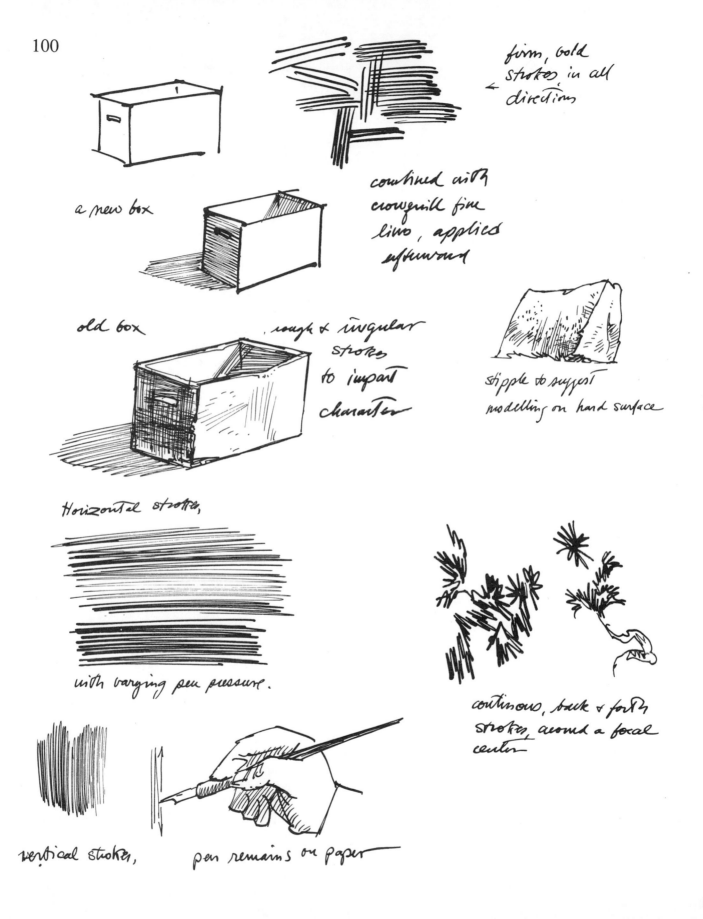

firm, bold strokes in all directions ←

a new box

combined with crowquill fine lines, applied afterward

old box

rough & irregular strokes to impart character

stipple to suggest modelling on hard surface

Horizontal strokes, with varying pen pressure.

continuous, back & forth strokes, around a focal center

vertical strokes,

pen remains on paper

Detail from a pen drawing by Marilyn Miller, contemporary American. *The Reporter.*

three sizes of pen points, each in its own holder, a bottle of black waterproof ink, another of household ammonia—for cleaning the pen after use—and a chamois penwiper or cotton cloth. New pen points should be dipped in ammonia and wiped clean before their first use to prevent the ink from crawling instead of freely flowing to the point.

Occasional wiping of the pen during use is desirable. A medium sharp point (say #358) will serve for most line work, even quite delicate lines, although a "crowquill" or other fine point is available for fine detail or light line. Select a high grade of plate finish pen-and-ink paper; antique papers are not good because the pen picks up fibers and clogs its point. Paper is available in single, double, or triple ply. Spiral-bound sketching pads of various sizes are to be found in the stores, some small enough to carry in your pocket.

There are excellent fountain pens especially designed for india ink. These, of course, are excellent for outdoor sketching and for other situations where it is impractical to carry a bottle of ink. Since these pens obviate the need for constant dipping, they greatly facilitate sketching. A device for holding pens in the studio is pictured at the head of this chapter [FIGURE 98]. Use either push pins or scotch tape for securing the paper to the drawing board.

Cut a dozen or so sheets of paper into quarters and make up your mind to waste them. You must cultivate an attitude of abandon; fear of spoiling paper will stifle enthusiasm and hinder progress. Each time you begin a drawing warm up first on these practice sheets. Hold the pen in a relaxed but firm—though not vise-like grip—which would cramp the fingers and stiffen the drawing. In this practice work use all the kinds of strokes you see in the numerous drawings in this book. Make side strokes without lifting the point from the paper, using an arm movement for this. Vertical strokes can be made with finger movement. Bear down hard on some, ease up on others. The pen is quite flexible; a light touch makes a thin line, pressure spreads the separate points of the nib and gives wider, bolder lines. Variation of pressure creates variety and interest. Vigorous, biting strokes have great vitality. Slow, deliberate strokes will impart a ragged line, one that is useful in suggesting texture. A fast whip-like stroke renders a taut, smooth line suggestive of action, tension, and movement, the kind of line that might be appro-

- pen held almost
flat on paper

cross hatch - if used sparingly lends variety.

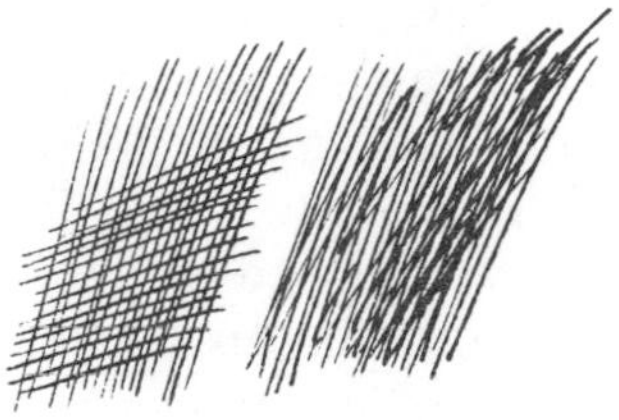

← outlined

102

a bit of right angle
cross hatch helps
"flatten" areas.
very light pressure

up and down, pen
staying on paper

vigorous,
biting strokes
very black

back side of pen
lightly held. for
hair line in clouds

see-saw strokes—
from left to right

103

Drawing by John Groth, contemporary American. One of innumerable notes Groth made for his illustrations.

104

Exact size drawing from life, by A. A. Watson.

105

Action sketch by Robert Henri, American, 1865-1929.

priate for the bleached limb of a dead pine, an iron rod, or a tightly stretched wire.

Tonal values can be produced by close spacing of either fine or bold strokes, vertical, horizontal, or at angles, according to the need, and by crosshatching. Crosshatching was used very freely and with great skill by Walter Jack Duncan but the student should be cautioned not to be too much committed to it. It can become mechanical and monotonous unless employed with the skill of much experience. Note how Herbert Railton, in his sketch of the Ponte Vecchio [FIGURE 118] achieves a complete range of tones with almost no crosshatching. Perhaps there are few pen artists with enough skill to handle the pen in such an orderly way; more often it is used in the free manner of Phil May in his "Guttersnipes" [FIGURE 117].

There are as many ways to handle pen and ink as there are artists. The Robert Henri sketch [FIGURE 105] is a fast-moving, spontaneous thumbnail drawing that aims only at expressing action; there is no concern with details. John Groth's sketch [FIGURE 103] is in the same vein, dramatic action without a lot of factual detail. The spirited sketches by Toulouse-Lautrec [FIGURE 115] likewise are impulsive action studies.

In contrast to such bold expression is the delicate line rendering by Sadolin [FIGURE 114]. Such drawings have a power of their own which has nothing to do with bold or delicate techniques. Power and noise are not necessarily synonymous.

Outstanding among American penmen was Charles Dana Gibson. Such virtuosity as his was the result not only of genius, but of the kind of persistent practice that is indeed characteristic of genius. With strong, biting strokes, pretty much without crosshatching, he rendered a very full range of textures with startling facility [FIGURE 116].

106

very rapid, bold strokes   lighter, still sketchy & rough.

107

Pen drawing by Charles Keene, English, 1823-1891.

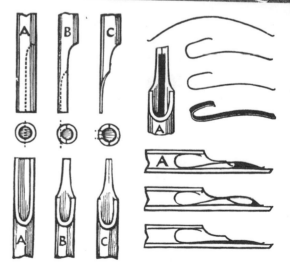

108

These photographs show John Howard Benson, American calligrapher, 1900-1956, gathering reeds, and cutting a reed in the making of a pen. *Providence Sunday Journal.*

The reed pen is made from the tall, bamboo-like reed that grows profusely in saltwater marshes along a highway. This is the reed *Phragmites Communis,* if you want the scientific name. More important is the fact that, if you are an experimenter, you can make pens that are extremely useful. Like the quill, it has individual characteristics that may please you. In Figure 108 the late John Howard Benson is seen gathering these reeds which he greatly favored for making manuscript pens. The picture beside it shows the method of cutting the reed with a penknife. The watch spring seen in this photograph is cut and bent, as illustrated, then inserted inside the reed to make a reservoir for holding a reasonable amount of ink—not only to prevent constant dipping, but also to insure a uniform flow.

Various point shapes are shown in Figure 109. These particular ones are for lettering, but the point may be whittled down much narrower. However, reed pens are not adapted to the fine work which steel pens can perform. The reed pen is for bold rendering rather than for fine detail. Something new is always learned from an unfamiliar tool even if it happens not to be sympathetic to the artist's temperament.

The *quill* pen is the drawing tool responsible for much of that luscious quality of line to be seen in the pen drawings of the old masters. It is a line that responds sympathetically to the artist's impulse for expression. It is flexible, ranging from hair-line delicacy to bold, broad accents. The quill gives solid blacks and beautiful gray qualities suggestive of the brush, all depending upon how it is used. It is smooth; the quill glides over the paper without effort. All of which any artist can experience for himself. For—when one knows how—the preparation of turkey quills is a simple matter. As demonstrated on this page, the first thing is to secure the right feathers.

109

Diagrams showing how reeds are shaped and demonstrating the use of a bent watch spring to form an ink reservoir. From *The Elements of Lettering* by John Howard Benson and Arthur G. Carey, John Stevens, publisher.

more detailed, careful line work

Photograph and diagrams from an article by Dean Fausett, "The Drawing Pens of the Old Masters." *American Artist*.

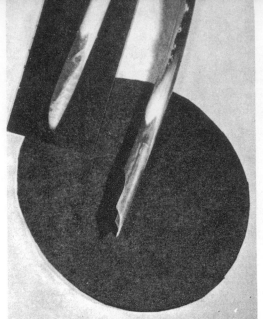

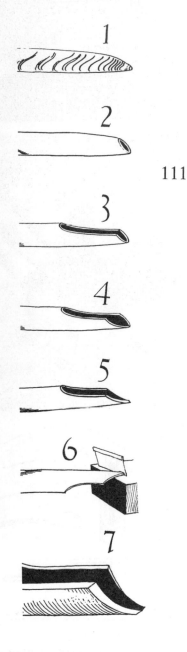

1

2

111

3

4

5

6

7

Quills from the wings are the largest and most nearly round. These are preferred to the flat feathers of the tail. Goose feathers are equally serviceable. Hen feathers are smaller and more curved, which makes them less desirable. The old masters used the crow quill [FIGURE 110] for very fine line work, hence the term "crowquill," applied to the fine-pointed steel pen of today.

Figure 111 shows the uncut quill and its fibrous structure within. After the first cut has been made (2) these fibers can be removed easily, leaving the quill ready for the next cut. Make this cut (3), not with a single stroke of the knife, but with two: one for each side of the quill. Hold the blade so that it cuts a bevel away from the center of the quill. At 4, one side of the point is cut back as a first step in bringing the quill to a proper point and in 5 the other side has been cut. These two cuts are made on a bevel as described in 3 and shown clearly in 7. At 6 we see a razor blade or sharp knife cutting across the point, trimming it to a straight edge. This may be narrow or wide as desired; the narrower, the finer the line produced. Note that this last cut is also made on a bevel so as to produce a chisel-like point. When not in use, stand the quills in a small bottle of water to keep them pliable and to prevent splitting. The watchspring ink holder or fountain described in making the reed pen can be adapted for use in the quill pen.

112

Quill pen drawing by Eugène Delacroix, French, 1798-1863.

113

Detail of a quill pen drawing by Dean Fausett, contemporary American.

114

Pen drawing of his studio, by Ebbe Sadolin, contemporary Danish illustrator. How satisfying is this sensitive drawing in pure line. Note the compositional unity achieved by the rhythmic movement of the emphasized lines of the tree, the vine, and the statue, all three lines gently flowing upward and to the left.

115

Henri de Toulouse-Lautrec, French, 1864-1901. From a boyhood sketchbook, published by the Boston Book and Art Shop from originals in the Albert H. Wiggin Collection, Boston Public Library.

The pen is a *small* drawing tool: bear this in mind when selecting outdoor subjects. On foot you will see many more likely subjects than if you ride about in a car. Large and complex pen-and-ink drawings have been done; Rembrandt made innumerable, rather ambitious pen drawings, and the Duncan drawing is a masterful example of this type. But a little study will show that he has skillfully harmonized several *smaller* pen-and-ink vignettes into a charming composition. When you stand and glance across an expanse of landscape, your two eyes may take in four square miles. But somewhere in that vast expanse is a smaller, unified picture that pen and ink can manage. Scan the countryside through your view-finder (described in Chapter XV) and a number of compact sketching spots will crop up.

Walk all around the subject, examine it, and size up its possibilities. Watch the light and shade, make note of any effective clouds behind it; you may want to include some in your sketch. Settle on the spot you like, unfold your campstool, and you're ready to go. Allow yourself perhaps a half-hour for the drawing. But before starting to draw, simply sit and observe the subject for a few minutes. Use as few lines as you feel are essential. Work promptly, but don't rush. As soon as you sense that you are wandering over the drawing looking for paper to draw on, stop! Consider the drawing finished, let it dry, and put it out of sight. Then move to another spot and begin a new drawing.

116

Pen and ink drawing by Charles Dana Gibson, American. 1867-1945.

117

Pen drawing by Phil May, English, 1864-1903.

118

Pen and ink illustration by Herbert Railton, from his *Builders of Florence*. Chas. Scribner's Sons.

119

Drybrush drawing by Stow Wengenroth, contemporary American lithographer. A fully developed drawing, typical of the carefully organized preliminary studies this well-known artist prepares before drawing on the stone.

IX *Drybrush*

The drybrush technique makes use of effects produced as the brush is running out of ink. As its ink supply is depleted the brush deposits on the grain of the paper a tone made up of very fine black dots which have the appearance of gray tones. It is obvious that the paper should have a suitable degree of "tooth," not a smooth surface. These satin-like tones afford a wide range of values which, in combination with solid blacks, provide charming tonal effects resembling the character of the lithographic print. So much so indeed that some lithographers, for example Stow Wengenroth, make drybrush studies preliminary to their work on the stone [FIGURES 119 and 120].

Good quality sable brushes are needed because this technique is hard on brushes. A poor brush will soon splay its hairs in such a way that it produces what is appropriately called "split hair." Sometimes this is desirable; it will give results similar to the effect seen in the drawing of the farm wagon [FIGURE 121]. An old split-hair brush is most useful. As you continue in drybrush you will acquire a handful of brushes, each having its special individuality and functioning with the others as a team.

India ink straight from the bottle is too thin to produce satisfactory drybrush tones. Leave the bottle uncorked for a few days to thicken it to the right consistency.

The possibilities of this medium will be discovered with practice. As we have said concerning other techniques, experiment, experiment, experiment until you have mastered this tonal art. The trial swatches here reproduced are offered as suggestions for practice.

120

This full size detail from Wengenroth's drawing shows the broad range of values he uses.

121

This drawing by E. W. Watson exhibits the special quality imparted to a drawing done with a "split-hair" brush.

In Figure 123a the black areas were followed by a horizontal stroke at the top before the ink had dried enough to produce the uniform gray tone below it. The tones in b were rapidly laid in with side-to-side motion. There comes a moment in the depletion of ink in the brush when the consistency is just right, and for a brief time a tone can be laid on with considerable uniformity. As the brush grows drier, however, only a limited area can be worked before dipping the brush again. All of these procedures are quickly learned through experimentation.

Drybrush may be approached in various ways. A more or less finished line drawing in ink may precede the application of tones, although there is some advantage in starting right in with the tonal work and using line work only for occasional accents. Another method is to rough-in the drawing at once with a fairly dry brush used in a sketchy fashion to establish the subject's general structure. Refinements are then built upon this foundation with solid blacks,

122

Full brush: tip laid on the paper, and stroked UP

Same brush, now drying.

same brush, drawing characteristic dry brush tone

tone first,
line drawing (with brush) added afterward.

a.

little finger supporting hand, dry brush back & forth – staying on the paper

2 strokes

1 stroke b.

8 continuous,
brush remains
on the paper

Wet brush

drier

Quite dry –
using tip of
the brush

just right
horizontal motion

even hair
lines have a
grey character

Vertical
strokes – from
left to right

tone worked over too much.

one, continuous tone. Leave it alone now!

124

lines and additional tones. Laying-in the drawing first with pencil is not recommended because pencil and ink are incompatible. However, in an intricate subject a few lightly penciled guide lines will be inconspicuous in the final rendering.

The drawing of the seated man [FIGURE 125, left] is shown as an example of poor timing; the brush was too wet and the tones are spotty and out of value, and they camouflage the construction. The strokes were laid on without reference to direction of drapery folds or the proper values of the book, clothing and face. The second drawing is more successful. The tones are so clear that the line work is permitted to function. The directional strokes on the shaded left leg define the trouser folds. Some white accents even within dark tones lend an atmospheric feeling.

125

Some of these lines drawn more sharply to bring out the drawing

126

Rapid sketch by A. A. Watson, preliminary
to a finished book illustration in drybrush.

127   A vigorous drawing by Norman Kent. The heavy black areas are supported by typical drybrush work.

Drybrush is a versatile technique for outdoor sketching. The sketch of the old house [FIGURE 126] illustrates how an experienced artist can more quickly secure line and tonal effects than with either pencil or pen. A broad range of values in its white-flecked tones give the drawing a lively sense of reality.

Norman Kent's powerful drawing [FIGURE 127] has a preponderance of blacks. Apparently there was no attempt at smooth tones in the gray areas; the rather spotty technique better expresses the character of this rugged subject.

The tendency of a drybrush stroke to darken at its end should not be disturbing; after all, this is a characteristic of the medium and it often can be exploited advantageously.

128

In these two drawings of cats, by A. A. Watson, the special characteristics of the drybrush technique have been exploited to suit the special requirements of the subject matter.

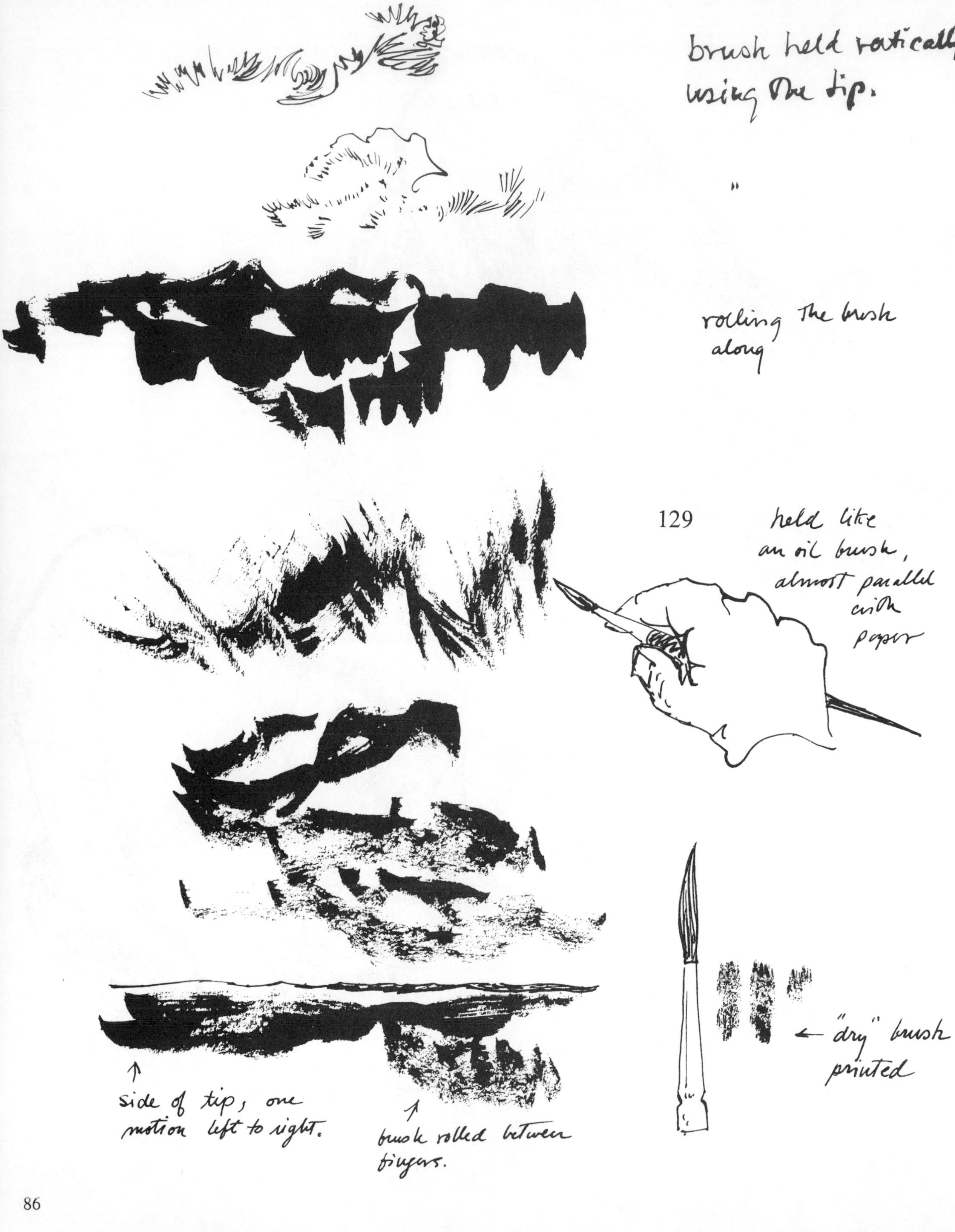

brush held vertically,
using the tip.

"

rolling the brush
along

129   held like
an oil brush,
almost parallel
with
paper

← "dry" brush
printed

↑
side of tip, one
motion left to right.

↑
brush rolled between
fingers.

No 4 Sable brush

X Brush and Ink

Brush and ink is a powerful and forthright medium. In spite of a quite different working point, the brush has a great deal in common with the pen. The loaded brush produces rich black areas every time it touches paper, and except for the drybrush qualities discussed in another chapter, its line and mass language is positive. Pressure is not as variable a factor in brush and ink as it is with pen and ink, since the bristles are very flexible. Although it is not primarily a medium for intricate detail, an extraordinary range of fine work is possible when a fine brush is used. Brush drawing is characterized by vigorous strokes, large black areas, and swift action—all in drawings on a larger scale than pen and ink. By its very nature, brush and ink evokes a simplified concept of drawing in which more attention is directed to masses than to minute detail.

This medium is admirably suited to outdoor sketching. The very simplest equipment will suffice: a block of smooth watercolor paper or bristol board, a No. 4 sable brush, a bottle of india ink, water jar and a clean cloth. Medium rough watercolor papers are also suitable when the scale of the drawing warrants it. For most brush drawing, a finer-toothed paper is best. The brushes should be washed in clean water after use, and pointed to retain proper condition for future work. Occasionally the brush should be rinsed in ammonia, and then water, to remove any ink which has accumulated and dried in the metal ferrule. Otherwise the hairs will separate and spread, making the brush useless. It is convenient to keep one nicely pointed brush especially for fine line work, and another for the

using the
point

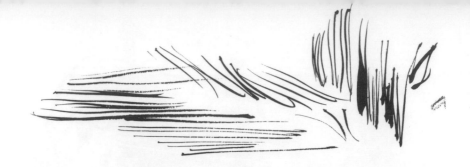

broad strokes—
side of brush

130

touched to
paper, lifted
off toward right

full brush
"printed" on paper

vertical
continuous
up & down
stroke —

full flat of
brush, loaded

heavier jobs. A band of tape around the handle will distinguish one from the other.

Working on some waste sheets, begin directly with a No. 4 brush and experiment with the brushing possibilities. Figures 129 and 130 offer some suggestions for practice. A natural hand hold, such as you would use for a pencil, will give flexibility for a wide variety of strokes—fine, hair-line, big splashy brushing, vertical strokes, side-to-side strokes. Although the brush can perform certain trick strokes peculiar to itself, we are here concerned with straight-forward handling of the medium with regard for drawing and composition. In these trials, the object is to see just what brush and ink will do, not to force it to perform like pencil or pen. Regardless of the medium, the drawing itself is, of course, of primary importance. These experiments will help you discover the brush's limitations, as well as its special charms. The medium is quite unique in one particular: a brush of the No. 4 size will hold a surprising amount of ink—enough, in fact, to very nearly complete one small sketch. This characteristic in itself will quite likely indicate the manner of your approach, and compel you to translate the subject matter into its simplest terms.

As drawing skill increases you will learn to call upon your brush for the special effect you want at the moment. As in nature itself, the eye is pleased by variety, so vary your strokes according to the demands of the particular subject; a uniform stroke throughout is usually monotonous. As your vocabulary in this medium grows, so will your ability to make drawings interesting in themselves, regardless of subject matter.

The question of leaving portions of paper untouched with ink is an important one. If you force the key of a drawing and let the white paper represent the lightest tone in the subject you will discover that your drawing is enhanced when parts are left "undrawn." This brings up the subject of design, or the effective balance and integration of white paper with ink lines and masses. Design and composition—for they are inseparable—develop with practice in drawing, and considerable supplementary study can be profitable. The work of professional artists, old and new masters alike, will yield valuable material.

One practical means of acquiring discrimination in the design of your drawings is to study them upside down. This at once eliminates interest in realism and focuses attention on the abstract pattern of lights and darks. Think of a drawing as something more than just a copy of what you see. Try to consider it as an art form. The fallen tree [FIGURE 131] is reproduced upside down to point out that design and composition may be more easily evaluated in this way. From this abstract viewpoint our sketch seems to need more delicate line work to offset the preponderance of heavy, solid blacks. The trial sketch [FIGURE 132] shows a method of scumbling-in a needed compositional element *while the sketch is inverted*, without considering drawing as such. Naturally, you may have in mind how it may then be translated into appropriate subject matter which will be legible to

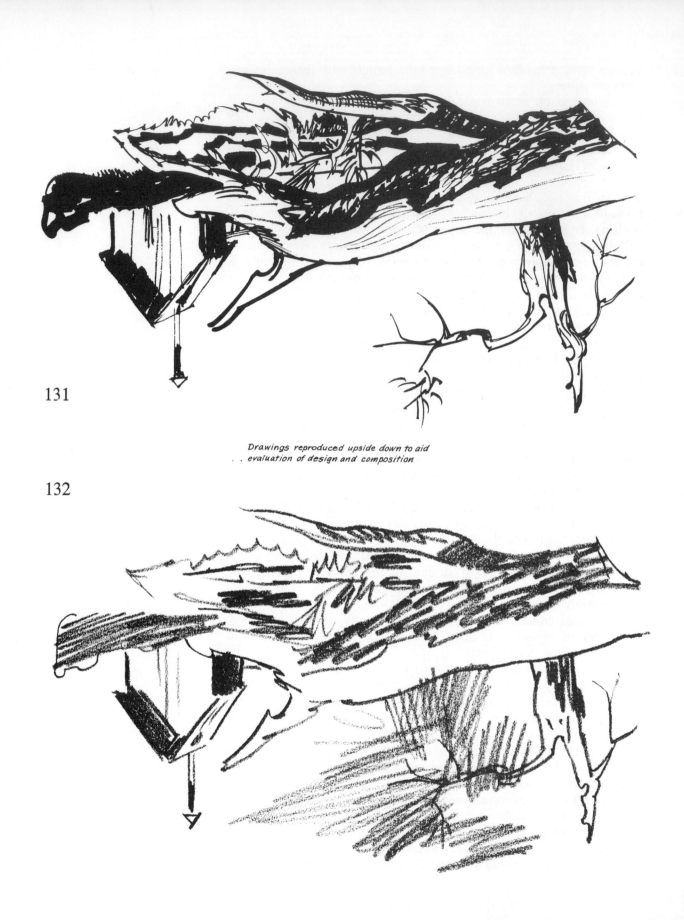

131

*Drawings reproduced upside down to aid
. . evaluation of design and composition*

132

133

the viewer. In Figure 133 the scumble has become a wild tangle of branches and twigs.

Looking at your work as abstraction may be a new idea, but doing so helps to develop sensitiveness to design. This type of training exercise is suggested as a means of learning that composition should be in the mind right from the very beginning. It is extremely valuable to make a very rough, crude preliminary without thinking of drawing at all [FIGURE 134]. This jagged sketch establishes contact with the idea, and provides a point of reference to which further drawing relates very naturally. Painstaking "filling-in" of black areas, covering all the paper, is pretty apt to result in dullness. Allow yourself a limited time for a drawing. Working at a crisp pace you will not have time to dawdle over detail that will weaken your concentration on the salient facts. Don't cover up those accidental whites! They add sparkle to your drawing.

Figure 136 is an example of a time-limit drawing. This three-minute note has very little detail. It is intended only to express the principal action. The top drawing of a man and his donkey was a two-minute sketch, barely a scribble [FIGURE 135]. In this kind of rapid note-taking one often catches the essence of life and action. The other three sketches were made on transparent paper over the first, to explore the advisability of adding more detail. It is often a question, after making such a group of trials, whether the first sketch may not still have more vitality. Take home a dozen crude sketches of this sort and redraw them on tracing paper a few times, trying

134

135

136

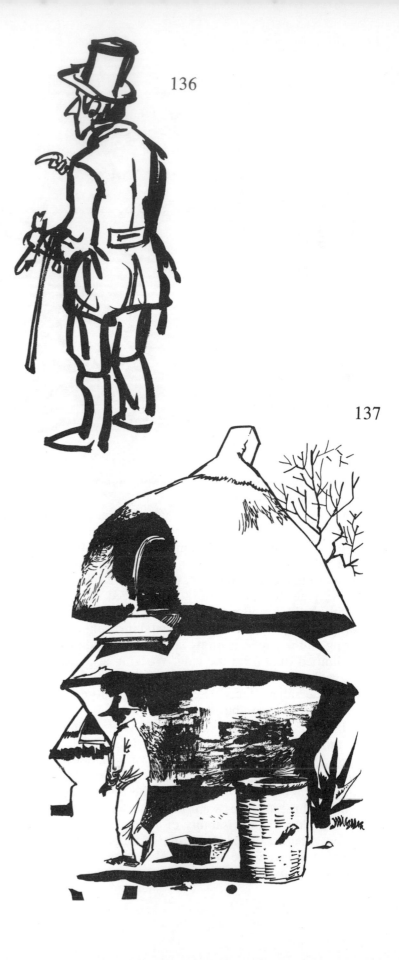

137

138

139

Henry C. Pitz.

140

141
Drawing by A. A. Watson, combining heavy blacks with very fine line work.

Norman Kent

142

Norman Kent. In this striking study a fully loaded brush has been used to record the salient facts. Note that the bold brushwork reveals a sure sense of foliage structure.

143

Henry Pitz. Although this finished drawing may have been the result of several preliminary studies, it has the artist's characteristic fluid, easy, and natural line.

144

145

146

various additions, but always striving to retain the spontaneity of the first impulsive note. This kind of research sharpens the observation, and increases one's control in future drawings.

Strong, contrasty brush work throws sunlight into a drawing. In nature, powerful illumination absorbs nearly all the halftones, leaving only the darkest tones [FIGURE 137]. In a situation which offers little or no chance for shadows, how is it possible to give the impression of light? The snow scene [FIGURE 138] for example, with shadows cast on the snow, would fade under brilliant sunlight. By using almost solid blacks, the effect of light remains. This scene on a gray day would reveal much more detail within the trunk of the tree, as well as on the board fence. This same principle is illustrated by Figure 139—a very quick drawing which nevertheless has a completeness about it, telling of a sunny day in the dead of winter. The small Henry Pitz drawing of a tree [FIGURE 140] is an exhilarating little chunk of brilliant day, yet there is nothing but jet black in the entire sketch.

Line work can be combined with blacks to fill out the range of values [FIGURE 141]. In this drawing, the fine line work conforms to the surface of the building, and delineates texture as well as value.

The Norman Kent drawing [FIGURE 142] exhibits a very strongly developed design. His use of the figure lends a dramatic scale to the scene.

147 Copenhagen Fish Market, by Louis C. Rosenberg, contemporary American. Pen and wash.

148 Winter Landscape, by Rembrandt. Fogg Art Museum, Charles A. Loeser Bequest.

IX *Wash*

Wash drawing reached a high degree of perfection during the Renaissance, when painters used this medium to prepare careful studies preliminary to finished canvases. The common practice was to make many fairly quick sketches, using a reed or quill pen with washes of sepia or bistre, to experiment with patterns of light and dark. There are literally hundreds of these handsome studies in museum collections and in numerous modern publications. Although this procedure was primarily a means to an end, these charming drawings synthesize many of the subtle qualities of both painting and drawing.

But wash drawing is a substantial medium in its own right and without a further end in view. The simple, monochromatic tones, judiciously laid-in, give a drawing substance and introduce very pleasing qualities of light and atmosphere. In Figure 147 the simple washes, in three different values, have created dimension and have given substance to the delicate pen rendering. Even so simple an application as the Rembrandt landscape [FIGURE 148]—a flat tint over the entire area—immediately imparts a *sense of reality*. Wash drawing is a versatile and logical adjunct to all line drawing mediums: pencil, brush and ink, pen and ink, and crayon. The wash tends to soften the harshness of pen work, flowing over it without crawling or picking up any of the preliminary drawing.

Combining wash with any of the line mediums is excellent training in judging the color values of a landscape. The subject's mood can often be accentuated by the use of washes, as in Figure

149
Wash drawing by Albrecht Dürer, German, 1471-1528. The Albertina Museum.

150

Deserted House, by E. W. Watson. Pen
and sepia wash.

150 where a few telling washes accomplish what would have been
more exacting and perhaps less dramatic if done with pen alone. In
Figure 151 the washes were applied *after* the pen rendering had
been completed, in order to draw the whole composition together.
The foreground was done in burnt sienna, while the background was
washed with sepia, an interesting color variation which suggests the
feeling of a full-color rendering. The tree at the left was given a halo
of wash to strengthen it as well as to silhouette the two buildings just
in front of it.

Sable brushes Nos. 3 and 4 will serve for almost any work you
are likely to do. You will need tubes of sepia watercolor, raw umber
and ivory black. At times you may prefer to use India ink instead
of the black watercolor because it will not be picked up by washes
which are put on over it. Two or three china wells—for studio work
—a water jar and a clean cloth complete your equipment. For outdoor sketching the palette of a watercolor set will serve instead of the
wells for mixing. Select a paper having some tooth or roughness.
Single-ply bristol board or illustration board are both very good.

151

Cement Plant, by A. A. Watson. Pen and ink, with washes of sepia and burnt sienna.

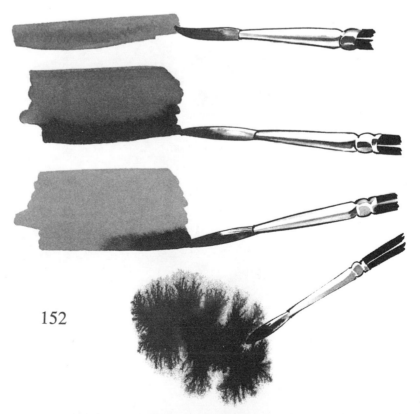

152

153

Pen and ink with wash. Drawings by A. A. Watson.

154

You will need to experiment a lot with wash effects to become familiar both with its possibilities and its limitations. If the area to be covered is large, the paper should be on an inclined board so that, as the wash is worked from top to bottom, a puddle of color will travel down the incline. The excess color which forms a pool at the bottom is removed with a dry brush [FIGURE 152]. Sometimes this puddle is left to dry, giving a desirable accent.

Strokes made in all directions should be tried, for it will not always be practical or desirable to put on flat, uniform washes.

Now make some trials on wet paper. First sponge the entire paper surface with a clean cloth and water. Then, using a full brush, drop some color on one area of the wet paper, and on another area draw with the point of the brush. Watch the effects produced as the paper dries. Since this wet-in-wet method requires some experience, its use should be limited to areas in which a tight control is not im-

155
San Giorgio Maggiore, Venice, by Hercules Brabazon, English, 1821-1906. Wash and gouache. The Metropolitan Museum of Art, Rogers Fund, 1909.

portant. If the paper is too wet, the wash tends to float rather than *spread* on the paper. *Slight* dampness will serve to just soften the edges of the brushwork. The practiced user of wash makes the most of this wet method, rendering both sharp and soft edges by manipulation of the variously drying areas.

The tree sketch [FIGURE 153] was first completed in pen and ink on illustration board. When the ink was dry, the entire board was dampened and the wash applied while wet. With practice, the extent of the "bleeding" (spreading) can be anticipated. The sketch with the dark sky [FIGURE 154] was done in reverse order; the wash drawing first, and the pen and ink work afterwards. Since bleeding of the washes was needed only in the sky, only the top part of the board was wet. The foreground was rendered on dry board. Some concept of the total composition must be kept in mind before starting a drawing with this method.

156 Saskia Ill in Bed with a Child, by Rembrandt. Reed and quill pens, with bistre and
green-gray washes. Fogg Art Museum,
Sachs Collection.

157　A Venetian Scene, by Francesco Guardi, Italian, 18th Century. Pen with Sepia wash. Fogg Art Museum, Charles A. Loeser Bequest.

The most casual or seemingly insignificant subject matter can be brought to life by judicious use of wash, as the sketches by the old masters indicate. Such, for example, is Rembrandt's charming drawing [FIGURE 156], which is a delightful picture developed with simple washes. Although Rembrandt epitomizes the most highly developed skill, serious study of this type of drawing sharpens our visual discrimination. In this homely scene, which offhand may seem an unlikely subject, he has composed a majestic tableau, quiet and dignified. In the drawing by Guardi [FIGURE 157] the pen work is very rough, and the wash has been used to rough out his concept of a composition which probably was later developed into a painting. Cambiaso laid his washes on a great deal more sharply, imparting a crisp effect to the drapery [FIGURE 158].

158 St. Matthew and the Angel, by Luca Cambiaso, Italian, 16th Century. Pen with bistre wash. Fogg Art Museum, Sachs Collection.

159 Youth Reading, by Pier Francesco Mola, Italian, 17th Century. Pen with bistre wash. The Metropolitan Museum of Art, Gift of Cornelius Vanderbilt, 1880.

160 Parker's Bog, by Edward A. Wilson, contemporary American. Wash drawing, from the artist's collection.

Wash can be manipulated to carry the full weight of a drawing—without any line support from the pen. Or the point of the brush may be used to sharpen the drawing detail. Masses of wash alone, treated like watercolor painting, may suffice for structural definition, as in the landscape by Edward A. Wilson [FIGURE 160]. In the foreground he has drawn the coarser textures of grass and foliage with the brush point, and made skillful use of white paper as well. Another example of this approach to wash drawing is the handsome rabbit by Dürer at the opening of this chapter.

161

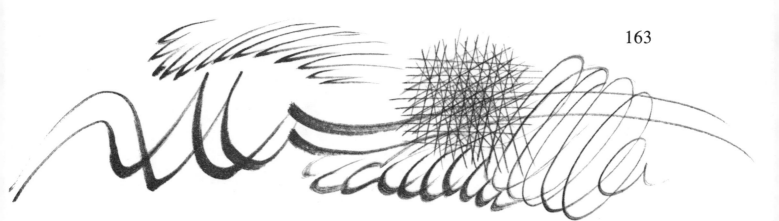

163

XII *Felt Tip*

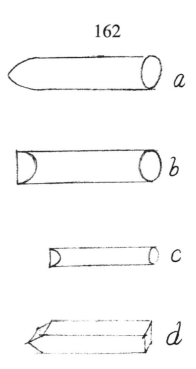

162

Do you want to have a lot of fun? Then get acquainted with the felt tip. Although commonly called felt-tip pen, the name "pen" is scarcely applicable to this tool which acts more like a brush. Felt tips of sizes and shapes like those shown in Figure 162 are inserted in a fountain holder resembling a fountain pen. The ink is really a dye which dries instantly when it touches the paper. As one begins to draw and bears down lightly on the pen, the felt is brought into contact with the ink in the reservoir and is impregnated. When the felt is soaked with the dye, the pen produces heavy black strokes such as the dark tones in Figure 165. There are times when this bold effect is desired, but the great versatility of the medium is not realized until the flow of ink has been controlled. The examples shown in this chapter illustrate the range of its possibilities.

The light gray effects, the delicate lines are only achieved when the flow of ink has been retarded. The way to reduce the ink volume at the tip of the felt is to squeeze it with a rag until it delivers gray rather than black.

Thus the medium will be found to be a bit tricky and somewhat frustrating until one has played around with it and brought it under control. The way to do this is to provide yourself with a lot of inexpensive, smooth-surfaced paper and blaze away. First fill several sheets with abstract doodles suggested by those in Figure 163. Do this until you have mastered the eccentricities of the medium. Then apply your knowledge to very simple objects such as an old barn or trees [FIGURE 161]. Do not be discouraged if you have some trouble

164

Rapid felt tip sketch by E. W. Watson. Exact size reproduction. The darkest strokes were drawn first; then with the felt tip squeezed semi-dry, the lighter grays were done.

165 Reproduced exact size, this drawing by E. W. Watson shows the power of the medium in subjects which permit a bold attack with some jet-black areas. The light, thin strokes were made with the edge of the same tip as was used for the black areas.

A Wyoming Butte

here. You will discover that this is not a tool for small-scale work. Although it is not as suitable for detail as other mediums, it becomes increasingly more so with experienced control.

Remember that mistakes cannot be corrected; once a line or mass has been put down it is there to stay. When things go wrong there is nothing to do but start over. This is excellent discipline, a sure cure for a tendency to "niggling." You just have to be positive, fearless, and impulsive; when you let yourself go with this tool you are bound to have delightful surprises. But your aim must be impression rather than careful delineation.

This is a fast tool, almost as rapid as a brush. For that reason it is especially adapted to sketching situations which demand quick work. As is true of all drawing mediums, you try to fully exploit the special charms of the medium itself as much as you aim to report the characteristics of the subject matter.

In discussing each medium we have put emphasis upon the kind of paper used, for this is often the determining factor. We suggested beginning your felt tip experiments with smooth paper because a smooth surface brings out more of the medium's peculiarities. Tracing paper is a most receptive surface for this tool. But a paper with a more pronounced tooth produces its own character,

Figure sketch by Henry C. Pitz. The original is 15 inches high. This is a striking example of the wide range of expression that is possible with the felt tip when the artist has mastered the technique. The drawing is on a soft-textured paper.

166

167

Exact size detail, reproduced from the Pitz drawing.

168

An analytical study of the light and shade pattern, from the drawing in Chapter VII (Figure 93).

169

A felt tip translation of Van Gogh's drawing (Chapter VII, Figure 92). Executed on a rough-grained paper, this sketch demonstrates a similarity of textural effect. Exact size of the original.

Drawing of a stone wall, by A. A. Watson.
The background pattern of foliage was
drawn with a very dry tip.

which may be desirable. For example Figure 169 was drawn on such
a paper in an attempt to achieve a charcoal effect. Figure 170 was
drawn on a rough watercolor paper. Interesting effects are obtained
when the felt tip is used on tinted paper. These drawings may be
heightened by the use of chinese white watercolor or with white and
colored pastel chalks.

As one becomes more proficient with this tool its remarkable
versatility becomes apparent. By using the width of the chisel tip
[FIGURE 162b or d] as well as its thin edge, and its corner, effects
like those in Figure 163 can be obtained with a single tip.

Do not overlook the opportunity of combining the felt tip with
other mediums. Since some difficulty with detail may be experienced, artists often use the steel pen or carbon pencil to add detail
to the broader effects of the felt. Charcoal also can be integrated
with the medium when a rough-surfaced paper is employed.

171

112

H.C.Pote

Exact size detail from a felt tip drawing by Henry C. Pitz.

Felt tip manufacturers supply colored inks as well as black, but a discussion of color is not within the scope of this book. In commercial art the colored inks are very useful. They also have special uses in the fine arts, and these the student may wish to explore.

We have said that this is not a tool for sensitive detail and delicate rendering. This certainly is true until one becomes a very skillful craftsman in this medium. In the hands of a master it can indeed be a highly sensitive medium as is evident in the figure drawing by Henry C. Pitz [FIGURE 166]. But, even in the hands of the most accomplished artist, it is especially suited to rapid and impulsive drawing.

Size is a factor here; as soon as one begins to experiment with the felt tip it will be obvious that it is better adapted to large-scale work. The figure by Pitz is fourteen inches high and the reproduction of his landscape [FIGURE 171] is an exact-size detail of a drawing about twice as large.

A fascinating aspect of the felt tip is its ability to render effects that resemble other mediums: ink, pencil, or charcoal, depending upon the flow of ink and the kind of paper used. However, its tendency to show black dots at the end of even the light strokes is a characteristic that is unique.

172

Studies of a Child and one of an Old
Woman, by Rembrandt. The Fogg Art
Museum, Sachs Collection.

Raymond Creekmore 173

Pen and ink drawing by Raymond Creekmore, contemporary American.

XIII   *Portrait Drawing*

Some persons have a more natural facility than others for "getting the likeness." This implies an unusually perceptive eye for discovering the factors that are characteristic of the individual, and the ability to draw them in proper relationship to each other. It is obvious, however, that without careful analysis of the basic form of the head and the peculiarities of its structure, the accurate rendering of features will not result in a likeness. Underneath all that the eye sees, regardless of its beauty or power, lies a bony skull. To some this may seem a gruesome object, but the artist regards it otherwise since it is the foundation of even the loveliest face [FIGURE 174].

In the young, and in fleshy faces of older people, the skull structure may be considerably camouflaged but the artist sees through the surface of muscle and flesh and begins his portrait with a consideration of its basic form and its individual characteristics.

While the skulls of all persons conform to a universal pattern, they present great differences of proportion and conformation in individuals. The cranium in some is quite spherical, in others it is elongated. The head may be narrow from side to side. There are square heads and elongated heads. Skulls with frontal prominence contrast with those that slope from front to back. The resulting facial angle [FIGURE 175] is a factor of particular importance in characterization; it is one of the first aspects of the head to be noted by the portrait artist. The undeveloped skull of the young is radically different in ways that are well-known.

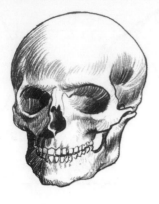

174

Pencil sketch after a woodcut of Lincoln, by Charles B. Falls, 1874-1960. The sketch of the skull shows how directly bone structure influences facial characteristics.

One can learn much about the skull by feeling the construction of his own head, noting the degree of flatness of the temples, the prominence of the cheek bones and the shape of the jaw. Photographs of all types seen in newspapers, magazines, and in reproductions of paintings should be studied in order to become acquainted with the infinite variety of head formations. It would be a good idea to make a scrapbook collection of these, along with analytical tracings.

Next comes the study of features. It is a good idea to acquire familiarity with these before attempting portraiture, or at least making a special study of them at the same time. Everyone can draw his own features and image from a mirror, and his profile or three quarter view by the use of a second mirror. Family and friends are potential subjects.

It might be effective to concentrate upon each feature for a time, making comparisons of individual characteristics. Modeling a head in plasticine is an excellent study method. Tactile knowledge is a sure way of acquiring familiarity with any detail. After modeling an ear, for example, one would not be likely thereafter to have

176

Drawing after the painting by Frans Hals, Dutch, 1580-1666. The simple diagram shows the basic form and the placement of the features.

175

The facial angle is an important factor in characterization, as can be seen in the two drawings by Alphonse Legros, French, 1837-1911. The Metropolitan Museum of Art, gift of the artist, 1892.

the hazy impression of that appendage which is so often exhibited in drawings by the less-well-instructed student.

If you also know something about facial muscles and the part they play in expression you will draw with greater assurance and authority. Some study of anatomy of the face will explain subtle but important lines that otherwise might be incorrectly interpreted. As you study your photographic collection referred to above, you will see these muscles in action. Caricatures—not cartoons—are extremely useful for study because they dramatize the play of facial muscles in all kinds of emotional expression. Consult the drawings and prints by Daumier, Forain and Gavarni. Look through art books in your public library and study faces in both paintings and sculpture; a fascinating and profitable research. The neck muscles should not be neglected because they are vital to the pose of the head. We refer especially to the mastoid muscles which attach behind the ears and to the breast bone. Do not hesitate to copy. You will only be following the example of the old masters.

It is assumed of course that the student will be constantly studying people in life. Television obligingly supplies a continuing

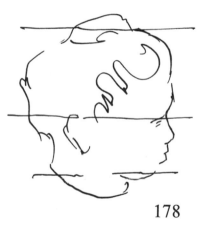

178

177

Head of a Young Boy, by Jean Baptiste Grueze, French, 1725-1805. Red chalk on paper. The original is 10 x 12 inches. The Metropolitan Museum of Art, Rogers Fund, 1949.

Pencil sketch of Armand Wargny, by Norman Kent. A preliminary study for a woodcut. Note the prominent cheek bones.

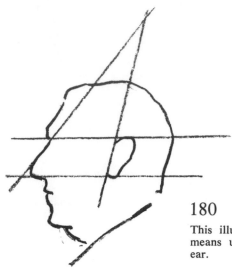

180

This illustrates a common, though by no means universal, relationship of nose and ear.

181

Gina, a charcoal portrait by Robert Fawcett, contemporary American. From *The Art of Drawing* by Robert Fawcett, Watson-Guptill Publications, 1958.

parade of models under perfect study conditions.

In sketching from the model start with the over-all form and proportion of the head. The analytical drawings on these pages give a clue to some relationships of features to the head form. The eyebrows, eyes, nose, ears, and mouth take their places in relatively elliptical, transverse lines that encircle the head [FIGURES 177 and 178]. Usually lines through eyebrows and tip of nose locate the placing and relative size of the ear. Regardless of variation in that respect this is a helpful relationship to keep in mind.

A three-quarter view of the model lighted as in the Frans Hals head [FIGURE 176] is perhaps best for beginners. The three-quarter view is most commonly chosen by portrait painters. When the sitter faces the light the modeling is much more subtle.

Charcoal is perhaps the best graphic medium for portraiture because of its flexibility. In charcoal one can sketch the head first in a ghostly manner, indicating form and features with very light lines and tones, searching out the sitter's characteristics. As the drawing reaches the point of assurance the tones are darkened with due attention to relative values and refinement of details.

In charcoal drawing, the head should be made nearly life size since charcoal lends itself to fairly large scale; the pencil will naturally suggest work at smaller scale. Size is a matter of personal preference; some artists naturally work large, others small. However the nature of the medium has to be considered.

It is important—through experimentation—to find the kind of paper best suited to the medium. "Charcoal paper" may not be the best paper for charcoal drawing; indeed many artists prefer illustration board, bristol board, or watercolor paper.

Kneaded rubber is the only suitable type of eraser for charcoal work. It is kept pliable by the warmth of the hand.

One of the problems of portrait drawing is the certainty that the model will fall into a lifeless pose. If you can engage the sitter in conversation as you draw, this tendency can be overcome to a

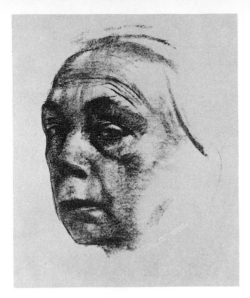

182
Self Portrait, lithograph by Käthe Kollwitz,
German, 1867-1945. The Fogg Art Museum.

183
Portrait of an Unknown Man, by J. A. D.
Ingres, French, 1780-1867. Pencil on paper.
The Metropolitan Museum of Art, Rogers
Fund, 1919.

184

Detail from a figure drawing by Robert Henri.

185

Cabby, etching by William Auerbach-Levy, contemporary American. The original measures 8 x 10 inches.

large extent. Naturally, it is not wise to expect your sitter to be still too long. Try fifteen-minute poses with five- or ten-minute rest periods. After working for some time on a portrait you will discover that you can continue drawing while your model is resting if you wish to do so; what you have been studying so searchingly will have been etched on your memory with surprising clarity. Part of the time you will prefer to draw during the rest period because this provides a chance to register one impression before it is overtaken by another.

If you are anxious to secure a good likeness of your subject it will pay you to request a second sitting. At the beginning of the second sitting, as you examine your work with a critical "fresh eye," you will recognize errors which previously escaped your notice. Perhaps also your work will appear to lack freshness, especially if you have used the eraser too much. In an instance like this, lay a piece of tracing paper over your drawing, trace the features, then transfer the tracing lightly to a fresh sheet of paper. A second attack based upon your first experience is likely to be more successful.

The portrait drawings reproduced in this chapter illustrate various types of treatment. It should be noted that the very meticulous rendering is not necessarily the best. Often a casual sketch projects the sitter's personality with more vitality. As a further training technique for portrait drawing, make dozens of sketches of heads in a small notebook, from people you can observe on the train or in the park.

It appears obvious that men are easier subjects than women. In men the features are generally more sharply defined. Old people are easier to draw than the young because the furrows of an aging face present prominent landmarks of both structure and character. Children are the most difficult of all because characteristics are not yet formed and the structure is well-padded with blooming flesh and muscle. For these reasons the beginner might be well advised to get his early experience drawing older faces.

186   Pencil portrait of Roy Mason, by E. W. Watson. The head in the original is about 10 inches high. On the facing page are two preliminary stages of the drawing.

187   Detail of a lithographic drawing, Two Heads, by Albert Belleroche, contemporary British. The Metropolitan Museum of Art, gift of Mrs. Francis Ormond, 1950.

188

Carbon pencil drawing by Norman Kent.
This figure sketch is typical of rapid drawing
from readily available models.

A simple line diagram, often useful for
quickly indicating the main action lines. 189

XIV   *Figure Sketching*

Self-consciousness in drawing seems to reach its apogee in the highly-charged area of figure drawing. There is a fairly common complaint, heard from even the advanced student: "I wish I could draw figures!" Two dominant problems foster this chill of fear. First, the fear of failure: failure to draw an accurate representation of the figure. The human being is an intricate articulation of limbs, bone, and muscle, whose proportions and variable postures necessitate longer and more diversified study than probably any other single subject. Because a model's pose virtually never can twice be precisely the same, one of the obvious requirements is long, determined practice. The second problem is fear of inadequate control. Even though the mind is willing, the hand falters. The slightest slip of the pencil may turn a beautiful nose into a roguish caricature. A related problem is scale. In some figure drawings the scale of the features may be quite small in relation to the size of the drawing tool. This mechanical obstacle can in time be overcome, and one way to begin its eradication is to start working large. But in either instance a confident state of mind will do more to sublimate these fears than anything else.

The purpose of this chapter is chiefly to demonstrate that anyone who craves the ability to draw the figure need not feel frustrated by the thought of first having to master a text on anatomy; he can proceed at once without even studying the book, although it would be profitable to keep a good one on his shelf for reference as the need for it is impressed upon him. Naturally he must gain as much

194

Pen drawing by Marilyn Miller. The "wrong" lines become an important part of the finished sketch.

195

Pen drawing by Joseph Papin, contemporary American. An excellent example of motion achieved through vigorous drawing.

first-hand knowledge of the structure of the human body as his opportunities afford.

The approach of the professional student will of course be otherwise; his study will begin with the nude figure—unless his aim is abstraction or nonobjective painting, in which case we have no suggestions.

The characteristic which animates good figure drawing is *action*. As you turn the pages of this book and examine the examples chosen for this chapter you will see that this is so. Some are drawn with greater awareness of anatomical structure than others; knowledge reveals itself in even the most casual sketch. But is it not evident that action is what gives them all reality? If you take up the word *action* as your motivation and are not afraid of trying, you will be surprised at the success of even your earliest attempts.

Another thing you will notice in these drawings is almost complete avoidance of detail. When watching the body in action, who is conscious of detail? How important is detail in a sketch of a cowboy on a bucking bronco? Do we think of the exact shape of his foot, the cut of his chin? Do these things matter? Actually, to be much involved with them in such a drawing would be a diversion, a weakness.

Proportion, however, can scarcely be neglected; the size of the members in relation to the body. Even here one need not be too meticulous; in contemporary art distortion is not only accepted, it is demanded.

The saying of these things is not to discourage the most persistent study of the body in all its manifestations. Obviously one cannot be too knowledgeable about it. Even the distorted legs of Fritz Kredel's "Cyrano" [FIGURE 207] tell us that he is thoroughly familiar with anatomical structure. Take every opportunity to observe and draw from the living figure, to observe creatively, to store images at times when drawing is inconvenient. Through intelligently hoarding in your memory impressions of people everywhere, you will find that they come to mind when you need them for future drawings.

Evening life classes are available in many places. And there is the beach. Every beach in summertime is crowded with people of all ages and types. Take an unobtrusive stroll along the sand with your pad and pencil. It is easy to make a quick drawing without arousing much attention. This is as good as a life class except that you have to be furtive in your drawing. Don't spend too much time on any one sketch. Pick out a figure, study it carefully, looking just for action, then jot down your findings in a few telling lines. Stop when you have used up your findings or when your model takes another pose. Don't try to "make up" in order to finish the sketch. Each unfinished drawing will add a little to your knowledge and your skill, even if it is no more than a scant linear record of an attitude.

Even if you are unable to engage live models for posing, there are plenty of photographs that serve very well. Drawing from photo-

196   Pen drawing from life, by A. A. Watson.

197   Duel Between Two Samurais, by Alexandre Jacovleff, contemporary Russian. A powerful crayon drawing that stresses action rather than detailed realism.

198 Pen and ink drawing by Lee Jackson, contemporary American.

199

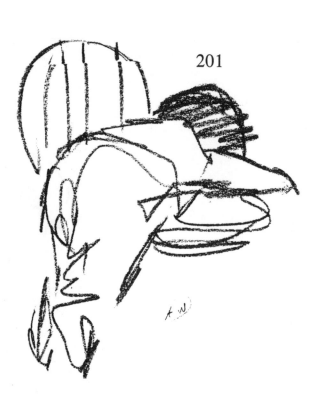

201

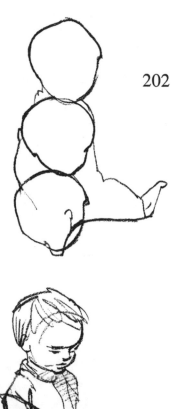

202

Pen and ink sketches by A. A. Watson.

204

200

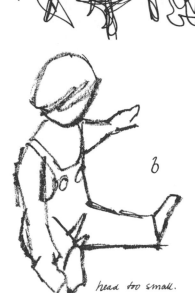

203

a

b

head too small.
compare size of child's head with
width of shoulders

c

better proportion,
but left arm
is too short

d

205

206

207

Brush and ink drawing, Cyrano, by Fritz Kredel, contemporary American illustrator.

graphs may be frowned upon by purists but there is very little anatomy that is unrevealed in today's pictorial magazines and you might as well make the most of it. It is entirely possible in this way to learn what a leg looks like in every position and from every viewpoint, even if you have never opened an anatomy book. But it is certainly a splendid idea to refer to one to discover what kind of muscle structure accounts for the curves seen in the photographs. No one should need to be reminded that television provides models of all kinds. Sketching figures from the screen is almost as profitable as drawing from the live model.

Soon you will be able to select instinctively the lines which carry the essence of the action, as Papin has done in his sketch of the boys on their scooters [FIGURE 195]. Note that his drawing reveals no apparent attempt at exactitude. There are many searching lines that fail to define or express. These remain to strengthen those lines which *are* significant. The same procedure is seen in Marilyn Miller's soldier [FIGURE 194], and in Lee Jackson's dancing man [FIGURE 198] who seems to be dancing right off the paper. The pen evidently was not lifted from the paper once during the drawing of the figure. This drawing method makes a special contribution to your skill. Try it. We are not suggesting that the beginner will find this "feeling out" attitude easy; it is something he will have to learn. But persistence will result in surprisingly rapid progress.

On a pocket-size pad make innumerable sketches in pencil or ink, from people on the street, in the park, at the railroad station—wherever people gather. The fountain pen referred to in Chapter VIII is perhaps preferable to pencil because it allows no erasing. At first this may seem a handicap; you will want to erase in order to correct, but the discipline of not being able to do so is just what is needed. For the sake of variety try all of the different mediums; each has something special to offer.

When you draw at home you have models who may be willing to pose for you, and at other times will at least not object to being stared at. Keep a large pad of newsprint at hand—about 14 x 19 inches—and a lithograph crayon or 6B pencil. The low cost of materials may encourage you to dash off ten drawings instead of one, and at the beginning quantity is more vital than quality. When wife, mother, or brother sits for you, the drawings might well be in carbon pencil like Norman Kent's drawing [FIGURE 188], or if preferred, in crayon or charcoal. Here you can and should work at larger size, giving yourself the privilege of erasing and correcting as you proceed. This is the opportunity for more critical detailed study. At home you can also make action studies of a member of the household preparing dinner, ironing or dusting, such homely activities as the old masters were fond of recording in drawings and etchings.

A good-sized mirror, placed on your table, enables you to be your own model. If you have a door mirror so much the better. While posing for yourself, you can take all the time you need to make meticulous drawings of features, fingers, and feet. When drawing hands and other details keep the drawing simple. Concentrate

208 Pen and ink illustration by Fritz Kredel from his *Anderson's Fairy Tales*. A handsome drawing done with typical force and assurance.

209 William Glackens, American painter, 1870-1938.

210 Drawing by A. A. Watson.

Cammie
Sept 26 1959
Cape Cod

AW

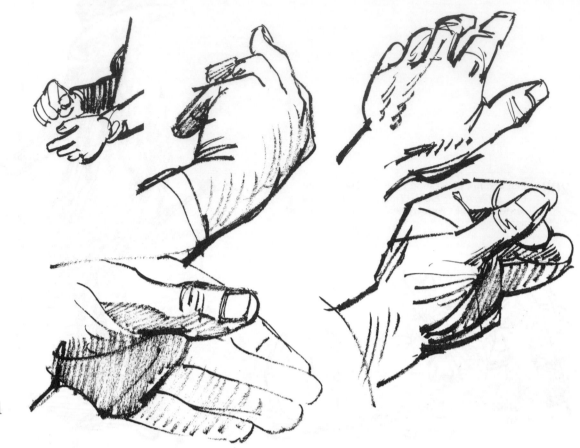

on the basic construction, not on fingernails and veins. Draw all the hands in the family: adults' and children's. Have someone pose the hand with scissors, a book, a pipe. In these drawings try not to use an eraser; instead draw corrected lines over them.

If there is a baby in the house you will want to use him for a model. Because he won't be still a minute you will be making false starts constantly, but if you seize upon the main action lines you will get some good drawings. You will very often improve your drawing by trying to memorize a given action, then sketching it afterwards. Learning to draw is primarily the training of observation, really *learning to see*.

Figure 203 represents the kind of experience you may have in early attempts. The first sketch (a) is a thirty-second drawing, crude, and without hands or feet. At this stage it doesn't matter if the head looks like nothing more than a ball. The next will show signs of improvement as you begin searching for more definite form. These preliminary "bad" drawings must be done simply to be gotten out of the way. In the second trial (b) the head is too small, and the arm too heavy but it has some merit. The third sketch (c) shows greater perception; it has caught much of the significant action. The fourth drawing (d) goes still further. In Figure 204 there is perhaps a more satisfactory conclusion. The point of these sketches is to suggest an evolution of development in a series of trials that are not

212

concerned with details and expression. So far as an impression of life is concerned, the drawing of the running boy seems a complete statement [FIGURE 206].

In drawing clothed figures you will become involved with drapery. The purpose of clothing being to cover the figure, its action must reflect the action of the form underneath. Study the "anatomy" of drapery, the way it hangs and folds under different circumstances. Some study can be carried out by draping different kinds of material over the arm of the sofa or upholstered chair. Fashion illustrations are your best source of models. But slavish copying of folds and flounces without reference to the figure seldom reveals the essence of the human anatomy beneath it. Examine the Kredel woodcut [FIGURE 207]. In this very bold brush drawing the whole focus is on Cyrano's character. There is enough costume to establish the period and that is all.

To extend your practice of figure drawing, acquire the habit of putting a figure into your landscape drawings. On a piece of tracing paper, laid over one of your landscape drawings, draw a few trial figures. When you have developed one which fits the content of the landscape, make a fresh drawing of the entire composition [FIGURE 212]. This practice may also improve your judgment in outdoor sketching; you may need to rearrange the compositional elements so that the figure takes its logical place.

213

Pen and ink illustrations by Gordon Grant,
contemporary American, from *Gordon
Grant's Sketchbook,* Watson-Guptill Publications.

214

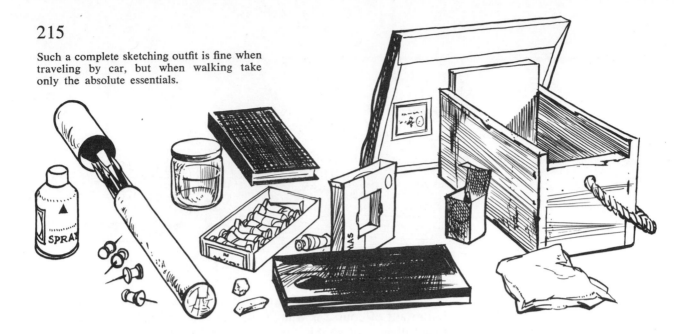

215

Such a complete sketching outfit is fine when traveling by car, but when walking take only the absolute essentials.

XV *Outdoor Sketching*

Outdoor sketching is one of the most rewarding experiences in the life of an artist. You wake up early on a summer morning, birds are singing; the sun, pink and freshly shining through your bedroom window. It's going to be a perfect day. What else can you do but make a lunch, pick out a few materials and set out for a day of sketching? Such are the rare moments of life when restrictions, requirements, responsibilities are left behind; when, in short, you are free!

A sketch may be but a few lines picturing your own inner joy. It need not be "finished," it is not obligated to say anything to anyone else or to sell anything. Even though later you may develop a sketch into a finished picture, now, at the moment, a sketch does not have to be preliminary to anything else. When you are out sketching you are just drinking at the wellspring, not knowing what inspiration and idea may come out of the invigorating draught. This is true whether you be amateur or professional, whether the drawings brought home from a day in the field are competent or incompetent.

In either case they record experiences that are beyond the capacity of the camera. Why is this? When sketching, one becomes a part of the subject, acquires an intimacy with it that cannot be conceived by one who merely points a camera at it. This may be difficult to understand by those who have not had the experience. Sketching is as much a matter of *feeling* as of seeing—even more. This sense of intimacy is communicated to people who may see your sketchbooks. They will linger longer over them than over an album

216

a

of snapshots because they are curious to see what you saw. More important of course is what your sketches mean to you: your pictorial diary will enable you to continuously savor the delights of many vacationing days.

The equipment required for black and white sketching is simple, inexpensive, and can conveniently be carried wherever you go. A light metal campstool, one that folds neatly to a flat 8 x 15 inches or so, is almost indispensable, and can be carried under the arm with a portfolio which serves the dual purpose of a drawing board and container for paper. Pencils or other dry sketching tools can be carried in a pocket. A folded newspaper is sometimes useful for those situations when a stone wall or a fallen tree happens to provide the most desirable vantage point.

If you want to be completely prepared technically you may provide yourself with equipment equivalent to that illustrated [FIGURE 215]. This is Aldren's sketching outfit; that is, when he goes by car. He picked up this box while beachcombing on Cape Cod. It measures 8 x 12 inches and is 8 inches deep. The sea had scrubbed it to a smooth, satin finish. A piece of flotsam rope serves as an adequate handle. The box holds a variety of mediums. It is kept packed, ready for instant use whenever the mood and the opportunity coincide.

Various drawing mediums are discussed in other chapters; here we are to talk about the creative aspects of sketching. Our chapter opened with a rhapsodical reference to the beauties of the morning. Indeed the morning light and atmosphere do seem to be made for the sketcher. But so does the late afternoon when the sun is low in the heavens. A low sun best reveals the beauty of landscape and buildings. The lights and shadows, more dramatic at these times, define forms which fall into attractive patterns that may be entirely absent at noontime. Students are sometimes advised to make several sketches of the same subjects at intervals throughout a day to become conscious of these factors. Those who have lived in coastal

A preliminary study for a watercolor, to experiment with light and shadow pattern.

towns, where fog often spreads its mantle over fishing wharves and buildings, have an unusual opportunity to witness the drama of light. At an early hour all objects appear as silhouettes, more or less flat masses, all details obscured by the heavy mists. As the sun burns the fog away, forms emerge. Patterns of light and shadow become distinct and details finally appear to complete a picture which one may be tempted to render with a pencil. Naturally some may be more intrigued by the foggy effects. In that event the medium is more likely to be brush or charcoal.

Thus we are reminded that these three aspects of subjects—*silhouette, light and shadow,* and *detail* are factors to be considered in almost every outdoor subject. Your drawing might well depend upon the collaboration of all three. Even when the motive principally depends upon light-and-shadow pattern, some parts of it can probably be effectively treated in mass silhouette. By silhouette we mean the over-all shape and character of any form. The dictionary definition of the word is "a representation of an object filled-in with some uniform color." The verb form uses the expression "to project upon a background like a silhouette."

We are concerned with both interpretations. Turn to Chapter XVI, where a number of trees are rendered in a single flat tone, unbroken except for holes in the foliage. The shapes of those holes are as decisive as the dark mass itself. Norman Kent, in his ink-rendered landscape [CHAPTER X, FIGURE 142] employed the flat silhouette with fine effect. In one of the two sketches by Arthur L. Guptill [FIGURE 218] we see an example of "forms projected upon a background like a silhouette"; although the darkened buildings are rendered with light and shade, the values are so close that they do not destroy the silhouette effect. In the other sketch, Guptill employed silhouette on the left side as a frame or foil for the tower group that is drawn in delicate line on the other side. In Herbert Kates' pen sketch [FIGURE 229] we see a somewhat similar silhouetting of buildings on the shaded side of the street as a frame for the

· Focus below ·   A. L. G.   · Focus above ·   A. L. G.

218

Pen sketches by Arthur L. Guptill, 1891-1956, American. A European subject showing two compositional treatments of the same subject. From his *Drawing With Pen and Ink,* Reinhold Publishing Corporation.

light-and-shade treatment on the sunlit side. This sketch deserves study; the rendering of the cluttered façades with their fluttering clothesline is a masterpiece of economical suggestion. One way or another the artist is always aware of the importance of silhouette. Even in such a delicate line technique as Sadolin's sketch [FIGURE 216] we are reminded, by the filling-in of the envelope that encloses it (a), of the well-designed silhouette of the over-all mass.

Thus the concept of "projecting upon a background like a silhouette" is a fairly constant factor in the creative artist's approach. From the start his picture or sketch is planned with reference to a containing envelope that unifies all the detail which is to go within it. It is possible that in Gordon Grant's pen sketch at Falmouth, Maine [FIGURE 213], the contour of roof lines (that is, the outline of the envelope) is actually as he presented it, but it is more likely that he *redesigned* it a bit to conform to an even more interesting silhouette projection. He would feel free to do so.

View of Fuji from Seven-Ri Beach, by Hokusai, Japanese, 1760-1849. The Metropolitan Museum of Art, Rogers Fund, 1914.

219

Silhouette pattern often appears in the picture's interior rather than as an envelope enclosing it. We see this in Hokusai's "View of Fuji" [FIGURE 219]. The orientals are notably pattern conscious; they like to compose in relatively flat masses. Their pictures are contrived as artfully as a poem: their artists seem congenitally incapable of the more casual attitude observed in occidental work.

Very often, of course, the silhouette is less important than other design factors; it may be wholly lacking when the subject's interest is focused within its outlines as in the sketch of a rocky shore [FIGURE 220]. The pattern here is one of sunlight and shadow. The analysis shows the basic shadow pattern sketched-in as a starting point. This might be called the drawing's skeleton, since it forms a foundation on which the profusion of fascinating detail was developed without loss of compositional unity. If a sketch is begun with no awareness of pattern structure the artist is likely to find himself confused and lacking in the confidence he should have as he works.

220

Rocks on Long Island Shore, by E. W. Watson. A preliminary pencil analysis of the basic light and shadow pattern, and below, the finished pencil rendering. From *Course in Pencil Drawing, Book I*, Reinhold Publishing Corporation.

221

Maine Coast. A pen and ink drawing by Arthur L. Guptill, from his book *Drawing with Pen and Ink,* Reinhold Publishing Corporation.

And after a skeleton pattern has been designed he has to be careful not to lose its integrity and become overly bemused with detail that is embroidered on it.

The pencil analysis of a farmhouse [FIGURE 217] demonstrates again how the sun often solves the pattern problem. In the watercolor of this subject there are variations of value and color but the outstanding shadow pattern is held as a unifying factor. The foreground elements in this sketch represent color differences and conformation of the land itself.

Designing the foreground of a sketch often taxes the beginner's ingenuity. We stress the term "designing" because suitable foreground patterns are not always found ready-made. More often it has to be "made up." Nature and man-made subjects supply at least the suggestion, but often the final arrangement must be created from imagination. In Figure 226 the stream and fence lead us into the picture, but in the scene from which this was drawn the stream ran horizontally; the artist changed its shape and course in order to provide a path into the picture. In the sketch of a deserted house [CHAPTER XI, FIGURE 150], the gate of the broken-down fence leads conveniently into the picture.

The problem is simpler when a path or road affords a perspective route into the sketch, as in Figures 213 and 225. This same treatment of the foreground can be observed in Rembrandt's "Winter Landscape" [CHAPTER XI, FIGURE 148].

We usually think of Rembrandt's work in terms of mass. His paintings are masterpieces of chiaroscuro, which is a mass technique. However, in his drawings there is an economy of technical means closely akin to the orientals, whose work he must have known well. In his "Winter Landscape" we note his consummate skill in saying much with a few active lines.

To a student who is trying to develop an appreciation of this kind of pattern we suggest an experiment with this Rembrandt sketch. Try changing it, "improving" it, if you will, by shifting the compositional elements around. Lower the horizon line a bit, enlarging the sky area. Alter the direction of the fence. Move the foreground trees a little to the left of their present position. These experiments will convince you of Rembrandt's instinctive sense of composition even in so casual a study as this.

7th Century Chinese print, from the *Mustard Seed Garden Publication, 1677*. The Metropolitan Museum of Art, Rogers Fund, 1924.

222

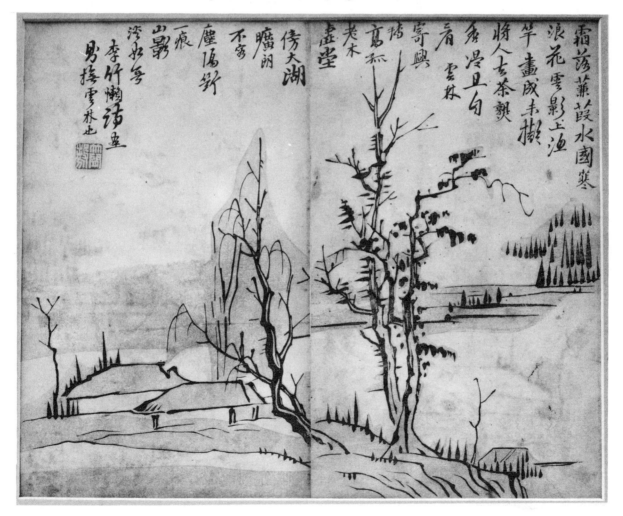

223

Scumbled mass layout for the pencil landscape reproduced below.

224

In this rendering, the structural elements—
trunks and branches—have been developed
from the casual suggestions of the preliminary layout. From *Course in Pencil Drawing,
Book 2,* by E. W. Watson, Reinhold Publishing Corporation.

Two sketches [FIGURES 223 and 224] illustrate how a landscape mass can be scumbled-in with a soft pencil, concentrating first
upon the character of the silhouette masses and later developing
both structure and light-and-shade. Notice that in the first sketch
the pencil strokes *feel* the structural direction of the trees' growth
while not attempting to be definite about the drawing of trunks and
branches. This is a most natural approach. Finishing the drawing is
a matter of picking out structural forms from the scumbled mass,
which at first were only roughly indicated. If the scumbled sketch
has been laid-in thoughtfully there will be enough structural suggestions from which to select shapes of some branches. Even in the first
scumbling one should pay attention to the character of trunk and a

225

Carbon pencil drawing by Norman Kent.
The original is 8½ x 12 inches.

few principal branches, leaving white shapes to approximate their direction of growth. Notice that the light-and-shade treatment has been left until the last, though even in the first lay-in there was recognition of shapes of foliage masses.

A very useful sketching device, the view-finder, is simply a small cardboard about the size of a postcard in the center of which a rectangular opening has been cut. The artist, squinting at his subject through this opening, is aided in the selection of that part of the scene which includes the maximum interest and will make the most interesting composition. It is most helpful thus to see the proposed sketch framed and isolated from the rest of the scene. There used to be on the market a metal view-finder having a sliding panel

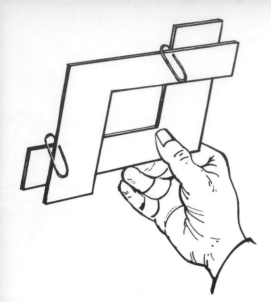

that altered the proportion of the opening at will. Students have made similar finders of cardboard. The simplest device is made of two half-frames which modify the shapes' openings according to the way they are held together.

In nearly every subject there is a point or area that is a logical focal point. The eye naturally seeks, and comes to rest on, some particular part of the scene. In Arthur L. Guptill's drawing "Maine Coast" [FIGURE 221], the observer's attention is drawn to the open doorway, both by the impact of its dark mass and the path leading to it. The boat also focuses attention. Try covering the door with a piece of paper. The path and the boat continue to take us to that spot. The stairway is still a compelling attraction. Cover that and the foreground as well. Where is the center of interest now? Or is there any? Do you think it matters?

226

Pen and ink drawing by A. A. Watson.

Perspective lines are powerful persuaders of attention as is well-demonstrated in many sketches here reproduced, but concentration of detail at any one point itself creates a center of interest even *without* perspective or tonal strategy.

There is an optical limitation in the functioning of the eye: its inability to focus upon more than a very small point at a time. We do not actually "take in" a picture at a single glance. This will come as a surprise to many people who have never had occasion to be aware of it. And certainly we are not at all conscious of it, because the focal beam moves over the area under observation so quickly and flits so unconsciously from point to point that the phenomenon is seldom noticed. Yet it is an important factor in drawing; it has to be reckoned with. To demonstrate the point hold a hand, with

227   Carbon pencil sketch by Gifford Beal, American, 1879-1956.

VOTIVE KIRCHE
•VIENNA

228

Votive Kirche, pen sketch by Gerald Geerlings, contemporary American. A fine example of "shorthand" sketching that demonstrates how a sense of reality can be suggested without the meticulous drawing of details. Only an architect has the knowledge to make a skillful translation of this kind.

Monroe Street
New York City

229

Monroe Street, New York City, by Herbert Kates, contemporary American. A remarkably facile pen rendering of a complicated subject.

230

Pen drawing, by Robert Henri. This shorthand record of a moving scene illustrates the great realism that can be achieved with such slight indication of forms; if the forms were isolated from the context of the whole drawing, they would be almost unintelligible.

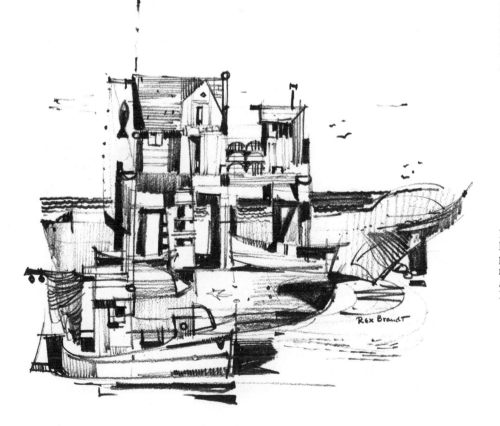

231

Pencil sketch of the Maine Coast, by Rex Brandt, contemporary American. The components of the landscape have been rearranged. From *Composition of Landscape Painting,* by Rex Brandt. The Press of the Rex Brandt School, 1959.

fingers spread, at arm's length. When you look at the thumb you cannot "see" the little finger. To do so you have to shift the eyes perceptibly. Notice your eye movement as you read this line of type.

Now it is obvious that recognition of this optical phenomenon is important to an artist when he is composing a picture. Knowing that the observer's continuously darting eye will have to move about in it, he naturally will want to direct his seeing, taking him from one point of interest to another in an orderly, meaningful, and restful way. Unless he does control attention that way, his picture is less likely to express his intention or contribute satisfactorily to the observer's pleasure: it will lack unity and thus may fail as a creative

232   Scene on Waterfront, by Herbert Kates. A broad and realistic effect accomplished with frugal means. Such highly developed skill in selectivity comes with long experience.

entity. The eye, put to the trouble of finding its own way, will of course see everything in the picture, but it will not get the intended impact.

One of the most frustrating experiences is to ramble in search of good sketching subjects and return home without having found a single one. The cause of this folly is the demand for a ready-made picture; laziness, really. This kind of fruitless adventure is familiar even to professional artists. Once, in the studio of a New York painter, we were admiring a recently executed canvas. The painter chuckled, "That picture is a sort of accident done late one afternoon on one of those empty wandering days spent searching for a good

a

1890

233

Two drawings of a barn: the first (a) as it might have appeared in 1890, when new. The second (b) drawn from life as it was in 1960. The line tracing of the dilapidated structure (c) points up the reason for an artist's interest in old buildings, which, in their sagging lines, present intriguing linear patterns.

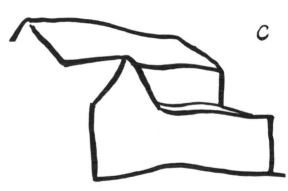

c

subject. Had it not been for a blowout on the crest of a hill over-looking this scene I would have returned home empty-handed. Getting out of my car I stretched and looked around before starting to change the tire. Then I saw the picture."

So often in exhibitions we see excellent pictures of subjects we would not consider worth painting. A fine canvas by Edward Hopper comes to mind—a picture of an undramatic railroad crossing in a flat, scrubby pine landscape that was as unlikely a setting as one could imagine.

Whether in a painting or in a sketch, it is what is inside the cranium that counts more than what the physical eye sees. You can make a picture out of anything. The measure of skill in sketching lies in how successfully a chain reaction is completed, how stimulated the brain, how fertile the imagination. You begin to find your-self adding, subtracting, substituting, improvising. The best sketch is not necessarily a representation of the most exciting subject you have seen, but a kind of song it somehow may have sung to a recep-tive imagination. The experienced artist does not try to tell *every-thing* about his subject. Like a good conversationalist he avoids boring his audience with wearisome detail; he seizes upon the sub-ject's aspect which first drew him to it, and by its development leads us to an enjoyment of its special beauties.

b

1960

234

Pencil drawing of an oak tree, by E. W.
Watson. This tree is a development of the
ink-drawn silhouette at far left on opposite
page. See also the analytical studies in Figure 236.

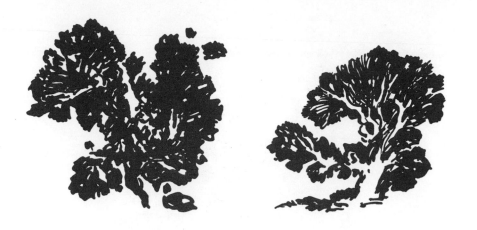

235

236

XVI *Trees*

A person who is well-known to us, seen at a distance, is readily recognized long before any detail of his face or figure can be seen. What identifies him is his form, or silhouette, and his characteristic stance or movement. The same may be said about trees. They have equally pronounced characteristics in form and in the way they stand, by which each is recognized as an individual. We refer not only to botanical distinctions that identify the elm, the oak or the pine. These of course are conspicuous; but each member of each tree family may be as unique as the members of human families; that is, after the tree has lived long enough to become an individual. When young, all oaks are apt to look alike. But after the buffetings of wind and storm, and after adjustments to the peculiarities of their locations, each will have responded in a personal way—it is not hard to think of a tree as a person. The oak that has endured the storms on a hill overlooking the Atlantic will be a distinctly different individual from the one that has lived in New York's Central Park. But even the latter will have been so conditioned by some peculiarity of its more sheltered life as to invite a nod of recognition by one whose daily walks brings him to its vicinity. They would recognize that particular oak from a flat ink drawing of it, such as those shown in Figure 235. Therefore, it is the shape and character of the mass that should first be observed and indicated on the drawing. There is no better way of approaching tree drawing than by making such little silhouette studies as a preliminary to tree portraiture.

Analyze and measure the tree bulk by relating it to some geo-

a

237

Pencil drawing of a New England locust
tree, by E. W. Watson. The small analytical
diagram (a) represents a simplified concept
of the basic forms within the foliage.

Traveler's Palm
Florida
1957

Ernest W Watson

metric figure; a rectangle, a triangle, a circle, or if a geometric figure
will not do, then a simple irregular shape like that in Figure 236,
which establishes the mass of the tree. At the same time, think of
the tree's stance. This is very important. Just how a tree stands deter-
mines its character to a large degree. Indeed if we miss out at this
critical point we cannot capture the spirit of our subject by anything
else we might do with it later. Its trunk may of course stand perfectly
vertical but, drawn by the sun and nudged by prevailing breezes, this
happens less often than might be expected.

    Having established both the tree's stance and the correct pro-
portion of its all-over shape, we next take note of the structure of
its branches and also the foliage masses they support. Referring again
to those silhouette studies, observe how few branches have been
chosen to support the foliage masses. Branches may appear light
against the dark leafage or dark against openings in it. In either case

238

239

Pencil sketch by Charles B. Rogers, contemporary American. The small diagram (a) illustrates the use of a simplified form to establish the tree's character.

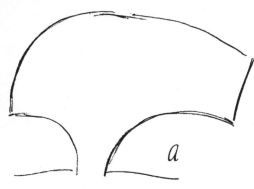

a

the limbs should appear where there are heavy masses to be supported, even though these may not actually be seen in the tree because obscured by leaves. However, a section of the branch is quite likely to be visible.

It goes without saying that some anatomical knowledge of tree structure should be acquired by study of tree skeletons, trees bare of leaves. The analyses of branch growth [FIGURE 240] help in understanding their structural basis. Drawing fallen trees or their branches is an excellent means of acquiring anatomical knowledge. Not all trees grow in exactly the same manner, of course, but with few exceptions the *principle,* if not the *formation,* is much the same. The way branches join their trunks is relatively uniform. Old trees are particularly revealing of anatomical structure because, like old people, their character lines are sharply defined. But twigs of interesting growth can be brought into the house, and also serve as good models. Make a collection of these for detailed study at times when outdoor sketching is inconvenient or impossible.

There is the problem of light and shade. When foliage is not dense there may be no pronounced light and shade; trees such as the birch and silver poplar present fairly flat patterns against the sky. On a gray day there may appear to be little light and shade even on a full-blown oak or maple, but there will be color differences that can be represented by tonal variations in a black-and-white drawing.

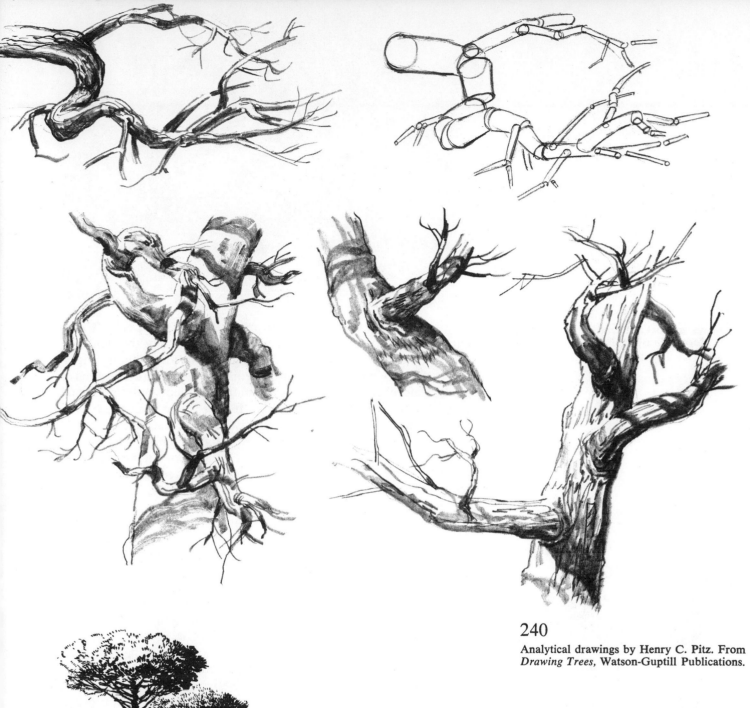

240

Analytical drawings by Henry C. Pitz. From *Drawing Trees*, Watson-Guptill Publications.

Via Appia
Antica

241

Via Appia, pen and ink illustration by Samuel Chamberlin, contemporary American.

Mares and Oaks, a Sumi drawing by Charles
B. Rogers. Brush and Chinese ink.

On a bright day the sun will mold the tree form and its principal foliage masses. It is a helpful practice to study the light-and-
shadow pattern in small sketches similar to the one in Figure
237a, simplifying and selecting forms that compose most effectively, before attempting a larger, more detailed rendering. Small
size is conducive to simplification. It is easy to over-model tree
branches in a tonal rendering; actually the light and shade on dark
leafage is less pronounced than it is on light objects. At the same
time the artist often represents lighted areas by white paper, as did
the author in Figure 237. Such a rendering does not necessarily dis-
tribute light and dark as it appears in the subject; it is often a matter
of design, the distribution of light and dark tones being purely arbi-
trary except for the necessary dark values that represent the shaded
depth of foliage masses.

Regarding methods of rendering foliage, everyone must find
his own way. Each medium employed will lead naturally to a
characteristic technique. In wash and in charcoal one works in
mass, pretty much in the manner of painting. In pencil or pen, suggestion will take the place of literal representation of tonal reality
because with point mediums the covering of large tonal areas becomes labored. With practice one learns how to handle the pencil
with the least effort to indicate what needs to be said about the
subject. This may be little more than line with a few patches of tone
here and there to indicate shadow or coloration, or even pure line.
Figure 242 Charles B. Roger's "Mares and Oaks" is an example of
Sumi painting, a technique that comes from the Orient. The medium
is stick ink, a carbon black compressed into a hard stick which has
to be ground on a wet stone before it can be used. The drawing is
done on a thin Japanese paper. This medium might more properly
be classed as wash, inasmuch as the ink is handled in a similar manner. The drawing is included in this chapter because it has much to
teach about the creative interpretation of trees. Note especially how
the two trees have been united compositionally by the rhythmic
"reaching" of their principal branches.

Pencil drawing by E. W. Watson.

For the artist, the study and drawing of trees is one of the most rewarding of his experiences with nature. Once committed to this pursuit, a lifetime of pleasure is assured. Like people, trees do the most amazing things. Dramatic differences in their character and behaviour are noted with surprising regularity, as one sketches them in various climates.

In Rustic Canyon, California, where this is being written, the sycamores thrust their trunks from the ground at fantastic angles, then take sudden notions to contort their branches in a way no living being but a sycamore could contrive. The live oaks, dignified with age, have a ponderous beauty suggestive of the extinct mastadon. Elsewhere there are trees like the weeping beech whose gracefully draping branches create a verdant waterfall. In the Arizona desert there are the Joshua tree and the saguaro cactus; in Florida, the palms and Australian pines; in New England—well, anywhere in this wide world where you happen to travel, there are new arboreal friends: surprising and delightful to meet and sketch!

244

Old Scrub Pine, pencil drawing by E. W. Watson.

An Old Scrub Pine
On the road to Christmas Cove, Maine, Aug. 1956.

245

Amsterdam from the Tolhius, etching by James A. McNeill Whistler, American, 1834-1903.

246

A thumbnail sketch done with a felt tip. Here the sky is a pure convention, viewed as an integral part of the Roman ruins.

247
Rock Promontory, pencil drawing by E. W. Watson. The clouds have been carefully designed to make this essentially a sky study.

XVII *Sky*

The first thing to be said about skies is that artists customarily give them scant attention when sketching in most mediums. In painting it is otherwise; the sky in any landscape *painting* becomes an inseparable part of the picture's color and composition, integrating with the colors and forms of the land. But that kind of interrelation of sky and land seems frequently to have little relevance to sketches made in pencil, pen, or other line mediums. The explanation is simple. If nothing at all is done with the sky, there it is anything—white paper. And doesn't that represent the cloudless sky which in many areas is as usual as one that is filled with cloud forms?

Herbert Railton made over four hundred pen drawings for his book, *Builders of Florence,* many of which are of building exteriors. In the reproduction of "A Pier of the Ponte Vecchio" [CHAPTER VIII, [FIGURE 118], we see the kind of thing he usually did with skies; a little patch of cloud serving merely to restrain the sliding movement of the roof line, and perhaps to satisfy the artist's desire for completeness. In Figure 245 Whistler certainly did not simulate cloud effects likely to be seen in nature. It is evident that he was concerned with design rather than realism. More often than not an artist is content to let a few scratchy lines or a blur of tone suffice. Claude Lorrain was satisfied to scribble a few lines and brush in some shapeless washes [FIGURE 249]. They suggest no attempt at realism; nor do Norman Kent's cloud lines in his sketch in Chapter X, Figure 142. In Figure 246 the cloud forms seem actually to lie in the same plane as the ruins and attach themselves to the walls. They

248

Pencil notation of landscape and sky, by Charles B. Rogers, for possible use in a painting. He has made hundreds of such shorthand notes.

are pure convention—not intended to appear realistic.

Despite these remarks which seem to condone ignorance of everything that happens above the horizon, no one will deny that an artist, whether amateur or professional, should become a serious student of the drama which takes place on that great stage. There will be countless times when he will wish to take advantage of cloud performances. Such an occasion was the day the author made his sketch "Rocky Promontory" [FIGURE 247]. Although the narrow stretch of land itself first invited his pencil, the cumulus clouds which began to boil up on the horizon demanded attention, and became the *subject* of the sketch. A photograph of the same clouds, made at any moment during the progress of the drawing, would be unlike those in the sketch. Nevertheless, those clouds were his models; the drawing represents the substance of their character rather than any one split-second appearance during their fleeting passage. You will discover that there are many subjects that practically demand a sky treatment inspired by nature, if not a reasonably natural rendering of sky effects.

When drawing clouds realistically you will be confronted with almost as grave a problem as when sketching the figure or animals in motion. Clouds usually move and change with such rapidity that an attempt to draw them with literal accuracy is likely to be frustrated. Although there may seem to be little movement up there, as

soon as you begin to draw, the cloud forms shift provokingly every time you look up from your paper. One has to work quickly, being satisfied to catch the great bulk and contour of the masses. After making rapid sketches of this kind one becomes sufficiently familiar with a wide variety of sky effects to introduce them into drawings without depending as much on direct observation.

With charcoal there is a better chance of success in direct transcription because the medium makes it possible to lay-in very rapidly large tonal masses, and as quickly take out light shapes with a clean cloth, a clean finger, or the kneaded eraser. One may do much the same with the brush (in wash drawing) after having achieved a reasonable degree of mastery over this more difficult medium. An example of this is shown in Figure 250.

Sketches such as the one by Charles B. Rogers in Figure 248 are typical of the kind of shorthand notations a painter makes for use in an oil or watercolor painting to be executed later in his studio. As it stands it would be a creditable sky indication for a pencil or pen and ink sketch.

This book is set in Linotype Times Roman,
a typeface designed by Stanley Morison
for *The Times* of London.
Text type is 11 point on a 12
point body, 26 picas wide.

Typography and design by ALDREN A. WATSON

Printed and bound by THE COMET PRESS, INC.